Charles Gibson

Knots and Splices

A Comprehensive Guide to Rope and Lines

MAYFLOWER
GRANADA PUBLISHING
London Toronto Sydney New York

Revised edition published by
Granada Publishing Limited
in Mayflower Books 1979

ISBN 0 583 13028 3

First published by Arco Publications 1961
Copyright © Charles E. Gibson 1961, 1979

Granada Publishing Limited
Frogmore, St Albans, Herts AL2 2NF
and
3 Upper James Street, London W1R 4BP
1221 Avenue of the Americas, New York, NY 10020, USA
117 York Street, Sydney, NSW 2000, Australia
100 Skyway Avenue, Toronto, Ontario, Canada M9W 3A6
110 Northpark Centre, 2193 Johannesburg, South Africa.
CML Centre, Queen & Wyndham, Auckland, 1 New Zealand

Made and printed in Great Britain by
Cox & Wyman Ltd, London, Reading and Fakenham
Set in Linotype Times

TO MY WIFE

ACKNOWLEDGEMENTS

I am grateful to Messrs Bridon Fibres and Plastics Ltd, rope-makers, of Newcastle-upon-Tyne, for their assistance in the preparation of this book in the form of advice, information and permission to use the following illustrations: Nos. 2a, b; 11a, b; 16; 28; 30; 33; 36; 65; 66; 67; 68; 95; 96a, b, c; 97; 98; and 99.

I am similarly grateful to Messrs Anglers Masterline Ltd, makers of fly-lines, of Tewkesbury, for advice, information and permission to use the following illustrations: Nos. 104 and 105a, b.

ILLUSTRATIONS

The line drawings in this book have been drawn and/or prepared by William Gibson.

CONTENTS

PART I
Fibre Ropes

CHAPTER ONE

THE CONSTRUCTION OF ROPES

1. Natural Fibre Ropes

Centuries ago men discovered that certain fibres, short in themselves, could be spun into long threads of considerable strength and they applied this discovery to the manufacture of cloth and, among other articles, rope. Up to the 19th century all rope-making materials were organic in origin – mainly vegetable. Today steel wire and plastics are more important but it will help in understanding the more recent materials if natural fibre ropes are described first.

HEMP Once so common a material for rope-making that it gave its name to ropes generally, hemp is now used commercially only where it will not have to bear a load. The best hemp rope is more than $1\frac{1}{2}$ times as strong as manila. It lasts well, is easy to handle, does not swell when wet, and loses little, if any, strength when lightly tarred. New, it should be a soft golden colour throughout, unadulterated by whitish jute.

JUTE This is used principally for cheaper twines and strings. It has a distinctive smell.

MANILA Made from the Philippines plant *Musa Textilis*, this is a strong, smooth, hard fibre rope which is never tarred as it does not rot when wet, although water makes it swell. Under load, it stretches up to 30%. New, it should be a light buff colour with no fibres sticking out at right-angles to the strands. It is made in Superior, I and II grades.

SISAL Made from the leaves of East African aloes, this is another hard fibre rope, as strong as Grade II manila, white and very serviceable. It stands up well to sea-water and, if treated, swells little when wet. Untreated, however, it may swell and be slippery.

COTTON New cotton rope is white, soft, smooth, smart and pliable but not as strong as manila, and once wet rapidly becomes hard, dirty and weak. Polished cotton twines and threads are much used in decorative work.

FLAX This makes very strong, durable but expensive ropes and is usually used only for high quality smaller cords, either alone or mixed with hemp.

COIR Made from the husks of coconuts, 'Grass Line' was cheap, very rough, very elastic, very light and only a quarter the strength of manila. It is now obsolete.

SILK Silken ropes challenge Nylon for strength and lightness, but they are so expensive that, although once used by rich climbers, they have now been supplanted by synthetic fibre ropes.

2. The Structure of Natural Fibre Ropes

If you have a length of natural fibre rope by you, examine it now. If not, look at Figure 1, which shows a hempen rope of three separate STRANDS twisted together so that, as you look at them from the bottom upwards, they spiral away from left to right. This is a RIGHT-HANDED HAWSER-LAID ROPE, typical of the vast majority of ropes in ordinary everyday use.

If, however, the strands spiral away from right to left, this is a LEFT-HANDED HAWSER-LAID ROPE. A rope with four strands, laid up right-handed round a central heart, is SHROUD-LAID ROPE. A large rope of three right-handed hawser-laid ropes laid up together left-handed is CABLE-LAID.

A rope may have more than four strands, either twisted together – which produces a rope smoother than, but not so strong as, three-stranded – or plaited, with the strands passing over and under each other. The latter is BRAIDED ROPE, which is strong, smooth and non-kinking.

Opening out a strand of hempen rope (Strand II in Fig. 1) reveals a number of YARNS, laid up the opposite direction to the strands to give the rope flexibility (except in certain specialized lines such as non-kinkable boats' falls). Teasing out a yarn reveals the FIBRES, which almost invariably have a right-handed twist.

Ropes for general usage are laid up with a STANDARD or PLAIN LAY, but others may be twisted up exceptionally tight and hard which gives them a FIRM or SHORT LAY; or more

Fig. 1

loosely than normal which gives them a SOFT or LONG LAY. A short-laid hempen rope is less liable to lose its shape through absorbing water but will be weaker and less pliable than standard lay, whilst for a long-laid rope the advantages and disadvantages are reversed.

Most hempen ropes are 'oil spun', i.e. treated with a special lubricant during manufacture to soften the fibres. The few which are not are termed 'dry spun'.

Hempen ropes intended for prolonged use in water are 'tanned' or 'barked', or treated with special waterproof dressing, but those which will be wetted only occasionally are merely soaked in tar. Tarring makes a rope stiffer and heavier and reduces its strength by one-seventh if firm-laid, one-sixth if plain-laid and one-third if soft-laid.

3. Man-made Synthetic Fibre Ropes

With the exception of polypropylene (see below) synthetic ropes are not made from short fibres, but from long continuous FILAMENTS whose thickness, twist and cross-section are varied according to the particular design requirements of a rope, a manufacturing control that gives them greater strength and uniformity throughout than can be obtained with natural fibres. However, this precision has the disadvantage that any distortion of the strands in a rope (e.g. when it is knotted) will have a proportionately more serious effect on a synthetic rope than on a hempen rope.

Synthetic ropes tend to be springier and smoother than hempen ropes and are therefore somewhat less easy to knot and splice. This is particularly true of monofilament fishing lines (i.e. single threads) for which special knots have been evolved (see Chapter Fourteen). When in doubt with any rope as to whether a knot will hold, take extra turns or 'stop' the end of the rope (see Chapter Three).

Synthetic ropes soften and creep as they approach their respective melting points (caused possibly, for example, by the heat produced by excessive friction on a part of the rope where one rope is drawn heavily across another, as can happen in a mountaineering situation, or in rendering a rope under heavy load round a post or winch barrel). This melting characteristic has the advantage, however, that a synthetic rope can be prevented from unravelling simply by fusing its end with a brief application of heat from a match or lighter.

Excessive exposure to sunlight also weakens synthetic ropes. Although this effect is negligible in comparison with the effects of wear, they should, nevertheless, always be stored away from direct sunlight.

The plastics used in rope-making are:

POLYAMAIDE (better known as *Nylon*) Weight for weight, this makes the strongest rope of any material (except, possibly, silk). A hawser-laid Nylon has considerable elasticity and may stretch over 40% under load, a very desirable feature where a rope may have to withstand shock-loading, e.g. in checking a climber's fall. It is, however, a disadvantage where a rope must not 'give' after having been set up, e.g. a halyard or a crane hoist. Nylon rope is smooth, completely free from rot or mildew, easy to handle wet or dry, and resistant to alkalines, oils and solvents such as carbontetrachloride, trichloroethylene, toluene, xylene, etc. It has, however, only poor resistance to acids. Although it aborbs water – which is of importance in fishing lines (see Chapter Fourteen) – it dries out without loss of strength.

Nylon is also used to make KERNMANTEL, a braided sheath enclosing a core of fibres, which is slightly stronger than hawser-laid and stretches only 20% but has a tendency to kink. A more recent development, especially intended for marine use, is BRAID-ON-BRAID, a braided sheath over a braided hollow-core (made in the UK by Bridon Plastics and Fibres Ltd under the trade-name 'Braidline'). The sheath and core share the load equally so that even when the former is worn, degraded or damaged, the rope still retains 50% of its original strength. Moreover, it does not spin, kink, creep or harden under heavy loads; it is soft and flexible, coils easily wet or dry, and loses no strength when spliced.

Another development for heavy marine work is the six-stranded Nylon rope constructed similarly to wire ropes (see Part II). Slightly heavier than conventional rope, it is stronger, low in stretch and resists deformation when multi-layered on winch barrels, but it is not made in any size below a 24-mm diameter. Neither are the eight-stranded ropes ('Squareline') of four left-handed and four right-handed strands plaited together in pairs, which never kink and wear twice as well as three-stranded ropes when used regularly round winches.

Nylon is also used to make webbing slings – for purposes as diverse as the heavy-duty lifting of loads down to supports for climbers. Such slings will not kink or tangle and their stress-carrying yarns are protected inside the woven exterior, so that cuts or face damage produce only minor losses of strength, as webbings do not rip. They should not, however, be used crossed or twisted.

POLYESTER (better known as *Terylene* or *Dacron*) Polyester ropes have many of the attractive qualities of Nylon but are slightly less strong. Their lesser elasticity, however, is an advantage where a rope must not 'give'. They are resistant to acids, oils, solvents and bleaches but not to alkalis, and have both a higher density and a slightly higher melting point than polyamide ropes.

POLYPROPYLENE Size for size, polypropylene makes the lightest synthetic ropes, though weaker than either Nylon or Polyester. Such ropes are made not from filaments but from either tapes twisted together or short fibres spun together into yarns in the manner of natural fibres. This latter method of construction allows different parts of a rope to adjust to simultaneous but different stresses (as, for instance, occur in a rope going round a winch barrel) because the individual fibres are relatively free to readjust their positions. Polypropylene is resistant to both acids and alkalis as well as to oils, but not to solvents or bleaches.

POLYETHYLENE (*Polythene*) makes the weakest of synthetic ropes but is resistant to acids, alkalis, oils and bleaches and largely to organic solvents except at high temperatures.

4. Steel Wire Ropes

Many metals can be drawn out into long threads called 'wire' but only one is of importance in making rope for general use: plow steel. Because steel wire rope differs considerably from those of both natural and synthetic fibres, it is described separately in Part II.

5. Small Stuffs

'Small stuff' is the sailor's expression for the many smaller non-standard lines which ashore would include packing strings, garden twines, cotton twines (sometimes polished and/or coloured) used for decorative work, and so on. Among the cordage listed under 'Ship's Stores' are:

Boltrope Good-quality, soft-laid pliable rope sewn to the edges of sails and awnings to strengthen them. It is made in various sizes. Sold in coils.

Ratline Three-stranded flax or Indian hemp used for heaving lines. Sold in coils.

Spunyarn Two, three or four yarns twisted together and usually soaked in tar, although it can be supplied white. The yarns, of flax or hemp, are sold in balls.

Houseline Three-yarn tarred hemp or flax, left-handed, it is strong and used for the serving or whipping of rope.

Marline Similar to Houseline but only two-yarn. Both are sold in balls.

Hambro' Line A three-strand flax or hemp cord, strand polished and tarred, sold in coils for heavy servings or lacing up canvases.

Log Lines Polythene, flax or untarred hemp, plaited and sold in coils.

Boat and Awning Laces Three-strand or plaited polythene twine, sold in hanks.

Leadlines 3 cm cable-laid flax or untarred hemp, sold in hanks.

Seaming twine High-quality three-ply flax or white hemp twine, sold in hanks.

Roping twine Similar to seaming twine, but five-ply.

Machine twine A high-quality, either two- or three-ply twine chemically treated to resist rot and mildew, sold in balls.

TABLE I

THE RESISTANCES OF VARIOUS ROPE MATERIALS

	Weak Acid	Strong Acid	Weak Alkali	Strong Alkali	Solvents	Melting Point
Sisal	Poor	Poor	Poor	Poor	Good	—
Manila	Poor	Poor	Poor	Poor	Good	—
Italian Hemp	Poor	Poor	Poor	Poor	Good	—
Polyamide (Nylon)	Good	Poor	Good	Good	Good	250 °C (480 °F)
Polyester (Terylene)	Good	Good	Good	Poor	Good	255 °C (490 °F)
Polyethylene	Good	Good	Good	Good	Poor	135 °C (275 °F)
Polypropylene	Good	Good	Good	Good	Poor	165 °C (335 °F)

Notes:
Natural fibre ropes have no melting point but are degraded by heat and may fail without warning.
Synthetic fibre ropes soften and creep as they approach their melting points, but give no warning of breaking when overloaded.

CHAPTER TWO

1. The Strength of Ropes

Any rope will break if you ask too much of it. Wherever possible, therefore, first check that your rope is strong enough to stand up to the work you intend to give it. Special care is needed when hoisting or lowering heavy objects, which is why the strength of a rope is expressed as the suspended weight under which it will break.

A rough guide to this BREAKING STRENGTH is that *new* Superior manila will break under a load, in tons, equal to the square of its circumference in inches divided by three. Thus, for a 1″ Superior Manila:

$$\frac{1 \times 1}{3} \text{ tons} = \tfrac{1}{3} \text{ ton gives the breaking strength}$$

Using the old Imperial measures, the size of a rope was given as its circumference in inches. Now that Britain has gone metric, the size is given as the rope's diameter in millimetres. An approximate translation is that 1 mm of diameter equals $\frac{1}{8}″$ in circumference. A rough guide to breaking strengths using metric expressions is given by these equations, in which 'D' equals the rope's diameter in millimetres and a tonne is 1,000 kilogrammes.

Grade I manila	$\dfrac{2D^2}{300}$ tonnes
Polypropylene	$\dfrac{3D^2}{300}$ tonnes
Polyester (hawser)	$\dfrac{4D^2}{300}$ tonnes

Polyamide (hawser) $\dfrac{5D^2}{300}$ tonnes

Polyamide (braid-on-braid) $\dfrac{6D^2}{300}$ tonnes

Using these equations, the breaking strengths for 1″ ropes (diameter 8 mm) will be: Grade I Manila – 426 kg (just under $\frac{1}{2}$ ton); Polypropylene – 640 kg; Polyester – 853 kg; Polyamide hawser-laid – 1066 kg; and Polyamide braid-on-braid – 1280 kg.

The guaranteed minimum breaking strength (mbs or b.s.) should be shown on any new coil or hank of rope or line.

No rope should ever, knowingly and deliberately, be strained to anywhere near its breaking strength. Even if it does not break, it will have been weakened for future use. Indeed, the *safe working load* (SWL) for a rope should be considered as only *one-sixth* of its guaranteed minimum breaking strength.

Remember, too, that the b.s. given is for a *new, dry* rope. An old rope will have been weakened by wear and tear and, possibly, by chemicals and, in the case of natural fibre ropes, the attacks of insects, rats and mildew. Many ropes are weaker when wet, including Nylon, which loses about 7% of its rope strength when saturated. Knots and splices also reduce a rope's strength by, as a working rule, about one-eighth, but this loss is not cumulative, i.e. if there is more than one knot and/or splice in a rope, the total strength lost is not the sum of each. The strength of a rope is the strength of its weakest knot or splice. Kinks in a rope and deformation of its strands also weaken it. With very thin fishing lines it is as well after each trip to cut off that part of the leader deformed by knotting it to the hook or fly.

2. General Care

1 If you have more than one rope in use at a time (e.g. jib, genoa and mainsail sheets, or two climbing ropes) you may want them colour-coded to assist in rapid

TABLE II

<table>
<thead>
<tr><th></th><th colspan="6">BREAKING STRENGTHS (3-STRAND ROPES)</th></tr>
<tr><th>diameter
mm</th><th>Polyamide
(Nylon)
kg</th><th>Polyester
(Terylene)
kg</th><th>Polythene
kg</th><th>Poly-
propylene
kg</th><th>Grade I
Manila
kg</th><th>Grade II
Manila & Sisal
kg</th></tr>
</thead>
<tbody>
<tr><td>4</td><td>320</td><td>295</td><td>200</td><td>250</td><td></td><td>330</td></tr>
<tr><td>5</td><td>500</td><td>400</td><td></td><td>350</td><td></td><td>480</td></tr>
<tr><td>6</td><td>750</td><td>565</td><td>400</td><td>550</td><td></td><td>635</td></tr>
<tr><td>7</td><td>1020</td><td>770</td><td></td><td></td><td>370</td><td>950</td></tr>
<tr><td>8</td><td>1350</td><td>1020</td><td>700</td><td>960</td><td>540</td><td>1280</td></tr>
<tr><td>10</td><td>2080</td><td>1590</td><td>1090</td><td>1425</td><td>710</td><td>1780</td></tr>
<tr><td>12</td><td>3000</td><td>2270</td><td>1540</td><td>2030</td><td>1070</td><td>2840</td></tr>
<tr><td>14</td><td>4100</td><td>3180</td><td>2090</td><td>2790</td><td>1440</td><td>4060</td></tr>
<tr><td>16</td><td>5300</td><td>4060</td><td>2800</td><td>3500</td><td>2030</td><td></td></tr>
<tr><td>20</td><td>8300</td><td>6350</td><td>4270</td><td>5370</td><td>3250</td><td></td></tr>
<tr><td>24</td><td>12000</td><td>9100</td><td>6100</td><td>7600</td><td>4570</td><td></td></tr>
</tbody>
</table>

To convert to Imperial Measures:

Size: Diameter in millimetres divided by eight roughly equals size in inches, e.g. diameter 4 mm = $\frac{1}{2}$ in; diameter 8 mm = 1 in; etc.

Breaking strength: 1 kg equals approximately 2·2 lb. To convert quickly, double the kilogramme breaking strength. This will give a safe, slightly under-estimate of the strength in lbs. Alternatively, 1000 kg (1 tonne) roughly equals 1 ton.

TABLE III

BREAKING STRENGTHS (BRAIDED ROPES)

diameter mm	Super Polyester (Braidline) kg	Super Nylon (Braidline) kg	Nylon (Braidline) kg	Polyester Matt Finish kg	Span Nylon kg	Poly-propylene Multifilament kg
4						180
5						225
6	650	950	350	225		295
8	1175	1450	675	295	905	565
9				565	1135	635
10	1800	2725	1125	635	1405	905
12	2575	3400	1475	905	1815	1250
14	3650	4300		1360		
16	4525	5450				
18	5675	7700				
21	7925	9525				
24	10200	12700				

identification. If so, it is unwise to colour them yourself. You may use the wrong chemicals and ruin your ropes. Leave this job to the rope manufacturer.

2 If possible, avoid treading on your ropes or dragging them over rough ground, rock or ice, or allowing them to be contaminated by chemicals.

3 Always properly coil ropes or ends of ropes not in use, as kinks will reduce their strength. Coil a right-handed rope right-handed, i.e. clockwise, and a left-handed rope anti-clockwise (Fig. 2a). Braid-on-braid rope, however, should be snaked into a figure-of-eight hank (Fig. 2b).

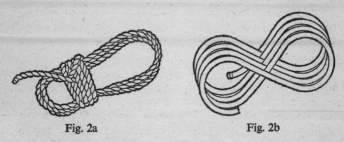

Fig. 2a   Fig. 2b

4 If possible, stow rope not in use by *hanging* it where it will not be exposed to heat, weather or sunlight. If necessary, cover it with an opaque waterproof sheet such as a tarpaulin.

5 Synthetic rope may be stowed away wet and will not lose strength, but hempen rope should first be dried in a current of air. If thoroughly saturated, it may never dry out completely.

6 When breaking open a new coil, read and follow the instructions on the label, if any. Otherwise, lay the coil so that you can lead off an end *anti-clockwise,* or it will kink. To remove kinks, coil the rope down anti-clockwise, pass the end through the centre, pull it from under the coil and coil down again. Repeat this operation – called THOROUGH-FOOTING A ROPE – two or three times. An alternative, if you have a boat, is to pay the rope out astern whilst under way, tow for a while and haul in again, coiling correctly. (All directions above are reversed for left-handed ropes.)

7 A hempen rope may shrink or swell when wet, so if you are using one for a guy or mooring rope, loosen it if it rains or at night, otherwise it may become too taut and break, or at least be weakened.

8 Do not use a rope through a block or pulley where the groove is narrower than the diameter of the rope, or has a rough surface or edges. The groove should support a third of the rope's circumference, whilst the diameter of the sheave should be at least five times that of the rope (and sixteen times for a wire rope). Lubricate the sheave regularly to ensure that it turns freely.

9 Avoid 'nips' in the lead of a rope, i.e. when taking it round sharp corners or over sharp edges. Where these do not actually cut the inside strands, they may unduly stretch and weaken those on the outside of the turn.

10 Where a rope is liable to be constantly rubbing against something else, protect it by parcelling (see below) or with a leather or plastic-hose sheath. Where it is liable to be constantly distorted, e.g. where a halyard passes over the masthead sheave/block in the 'hoisted' position, put on a tight serving (see below). Where it is in constant use over a period, vary the points where it passes through blocks, etc., and, if possible, occasionally turn it end to end to reverse all stresses.

11 Never allow the end of a rope to become unravelled. With synthetic ropes all that is necessary is to heat-fuse the end (but be careful not to damage any other part of the rope). The end of a hempen rope, however, must be whipped, back-spliced or pointed. With any rope, a quick temporary way to stop unravelling is to tie an Overhand Knot in the end (see next chapter).

12 Periodically inspect your rope(s). This is vital if you wish to be able to depend on them. Each rope should be run out, preferably on a table, and inspected a foot at a time by running it through the hands and rotating it to inspect all sides, including the inside. Look for:

(a) *Fibre deterioration.* Is the fibre breaking up? Does it appear to be dusty? This is often a sign that it has been overstrained.

(b) *External wear.* Are the crown strands badly worn? Or cut? Do not confuse this with the 'furring' that occurs on the surfaces of synthetic ropes as this is quite normal.

(c) *Local abrasion.* Are there severe chafes or plucked sections? Have kinks been pulled out causing the strands to hockle? With synthetic ropes, have any of the strands fused together, producing beads, globules or a hard glazed skin?

(d) *Internal wear.* The strands of a rope can be twisted open by hand but a larger rope must be opened with a fid (a wooden spike) or, if none is available, by a steel marline spike. Look for excessive powdering, and in natural fibre ropes for soft, brittle fibres or a charred heart. Mildew has a pungent smell. Rust-coloured fibres in manila and hemp and a greyish tinge in coir are warning signs. Overstrained Nylon becomes stiff and hard.

(e) *Rope that has been attacked* by acids, alkalis, solvents (e.g. white spirit, xylene, metacresol or wet paint), coal tar or paint strippers. This must be thoroughly washed with water.

(f) *Thimbles* (see Chapter Seven) – in a synthetic rope these may have become slack. Retighten the eye with a seizing round the throat with a strong man-made fibre cord, and check that the thimble itself has not been damaged or distorted.

(g) *To accept or reject?* The rule is: 'If in doubt, scrap the rope or relegate it to less arduous duties.' Remember that mechanical damage such as chafing and cutting has a more drastic effect on the strength of small ropes than of large ones. If only part of a rope is badly worn or damaged, this can be cut out and the two sound parts re-joined by a splice, with a loss of one-eighth in the original strength of the rope except in braid-on-braid.

3. Whipping the End of a Rope

Whipping is binding the rope with twine, preferably waxed on a hempen rope, or synthetic on a man-made fibre rope. Whatever type of whipping is used, the binding must be tight and, if working at the end of a rope, must start away from the end and work towards it. Here its length should be about equal to the circumference of the rope.

To make a COMMON WHIPPING *1.* Lay the non-working end of the twine along the rope to beyond its end if that is where the whipping is to be. *2.* With the working end, bind over the non-working end against the lay of the rope until within four or five turns of the end of the desired whipping. *3.* Bring the non-working end back to rest on the turns you have already put on and hold it in place with your thumb, leaving a bight of twine over that part (or end) of the rope as yet unwhipped. *4.* Continue with four or five more turns with the working end. *5.* Pass the working end through the still-uncovered bight of the non-working end. *6.* Pull on the latter so that you pull through the bight, bringing with it the working end. Both ends will now be together. *7.* Cut off both ends close.

A Common Whipping can be used in numerous situations where a smooth binding of twine or cord is required, e.g. on a fishing rod or float or on the handle of a bag.

A WEST COUNTRY WHIPPING is quicker to put on but not so neat. *1.* Middle the twine on the rope. *2.* Take the ends round opposite ways, half-knotting them every time they meet. *3.* Finish with a Reef Knot and cut off.

A SAILMAKER'S WHIPPING will stand harder wear than a Common Whipping and look neater. *1.* Unlay the rope for about two inches. *2.* With the strands pointing upwards, drop a loose loop of twine over one strand, bring the ends back between the other two, and make one end longer than the other (Fig. 3). *3.* Holding the loop and ends with one hand, relay the rope with the other. *4.* Bind the long end of twine against the lay into a tight whipping of the length required. *5.* Pass the loop over the *top* of the strand it already encircles and pull tight by the short end. *6.* Pass the short end up the only groove between strands not already occupied by a portion of twine and reef knot it to the long end in the middle of the rope. Cut off ends.

Whipping a four-stranded rope requires *two* loops, each around a different strand. Otherwise proceed as above, but when pulling taut, pull on one loop to tighten the other and then on the short end.

A PALM AND NEEDLE WHIPPING is the strongest of all. It requires the use of a Sailmaker's Palm (a leather strap that fits round the hand with a thimble built-into it so positioned that it fits in the palm) and a strong needle. *1.* Stitch through the rope to anchor the twine. *2.* Bind over the rope and the non-working end for the required distance. *3.* Stitch

Fig. 3

through the rope again. *4.* Take the twine down one groove. *5.* Stitch through one of the adjoining strands to the next groove. *6.* Take the twine up this groove. *7.* Stitch through the next strand to the next groove. *8.* Pass the twine down the third groove and stitch through the third strand back to the first groove. *9.* Repeat stages *5* to *8*. *10.* Finish with two anchoring stitches through the rope and cut off.

SNAKING is a way of adding security and decoration to a Common Whipping. *1.* After the whipping has been put on, stitch the twine through the rope and pass it round once, zigzagging back and forth across the whipping, taking the needle alternately under and over the top and bottom strands. *2.* Stitch back through the rope and cut off.

Pointing a Rope and putting on a COACH WHIPPING are described in Chapter Fifteen.

4. *Worming, Parcelling and Serving*

These three operations which often, but not invariably, go together are all illustrated in Figure 4.

WORMING makes the surface of a rope smooth and ready for parcelling. Simply bind spunyarn or some other small cord into the hollows between the strands.

PARCELLING gives a firm surface for serving and also prevents chafing, and water from entering the rope. For this last reason, on a vertical rope it should start from the bottom and work upwards. Simply bind strips of (waterproof) cloth some 5 to 6 cm wide round the rope *with the lay* so that each turn overlaps its predecessor.

SERVING, the final protective surface, is spunyarn or some other cord – synthetic on synthetic rope – closely bound round the rope *against the lay*. It must be put on tightly and is therefore better done with a SERVING MALLET (Fig. 4) than by hand; and also more easily by two people than by one, as one can pass the ball of yarn whilst the other puts on the turns with the mallet. A serving should be put on and finished off like a Common Whipping.

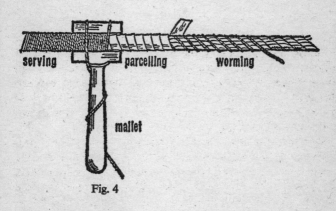

serving   parcelling   worming

mallet

Fig. 4

Remember: 'Worm and parcel with the lay
But always serve the other way.'

CHAPTER THREE

A good working knot has three qualities: it is simple and quick to tie; it does not slip when subjected to strain; and it does not jam, i.e. after being subjected to strain it is still relatively easy to untie.

1. The Jamming Turn

A hitch holds because of the friction set up between surfaces of rope pressed together, which is why hitches in springy and/or slippery rope or wire are not so efficient. A simple ROUND TURN of rope taken round a post, bollard, tree or bed leg (in some domestic circumstances) will resist a considerable pull if the end is held by hand, and more than one turn will offer proportionately greater resistance. A Round Turn can be surged or rendered by easing off the hand-held end, thus allowing the controlled lowering of a heavy weight or easing of a strain if no better equipment is available.

Fig. 5

FIGURE-OF-EIGHTING round two posts, a belaying pin or a cleat is even more efficient, especially if the last turn is taken as a JAMMING TURN. Figure 5 shows a rope figure-of-eighted round a cleat with the last turn jammed, i.e. that part of the rope on to which the strain is coming, called the STAND-

ING PART, rides over the part furthest removed from strain, called in this book the LOOSE END (but sometimes also the free end or non-working end). Now the greater the strain on the standing part, the more tightly it will press down on the loose end and prevent it from slipping.

But, *be warned*. It is dangerous to take such a turn with a rope that may need to be freed in a hurry, e.g. the sheet of a sail; for it may have jammed so tightly as to defy quick release. In these circumstances extra security then must be gained by increasing the number of turns taken and by omitting the jamming turn.

Taking the jamming turn off the cleat reveals simply a loop (Fig. 6) consisting of: the loose end (here, and elsewhere, shown whipped to aid identification); a loop or BIGHT; and the standing part crossing the loose end. This loop is the basis of most hitches.

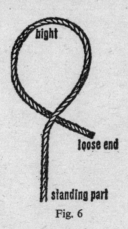

Fig. 6

2. Hitches on a Hook

The quickest way to secure a rope's end to a hook is to use a BLACKWALL HITCH as shown in Figure 7. The basic loop round a hook's neck holds more firmly than the illustration would suggest when under load, but may slip off when the rope slackens. If the rope is slippery pull the underneath

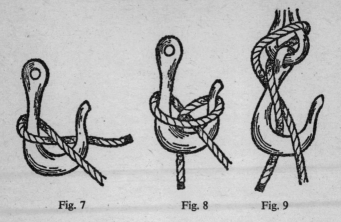

Fig. 7   Fig. 8   Fig. 9

part forward over the bill to make a MIDSHIPMAN'S HITCH (Fig. 8).

A DOUBLE BLACKWALL HITCH is safer still. *1.* Place the bight of the rope across the strop or shackle to which the hook is attached. *2.* Cross the parts behind the strop/shackle and back to cross again in the hook itself, with the standing part above the loose end at both crossings. (In Figures 7, 8 and 9 the loose end has been curtailed for easier illustration, and for safety should be longer than is shown.)

3. Stopper Knots

Stopper knots are put on a rope either: to stop the end from unravelling; to prevent it unreeving through a block; to provide a handgrip; or to stop another knot from slipping. Simplest is the OVERHAND (OR THUMB) KNOT. Make the basic loop, pass the end up through the bight and pull taut (Fig. 10). Taking the loose end round the standing part before passing it through the bight makes a FIGURE-OF-EIGHT KNOT (Fig. 11a), but more suitable for a synthetic rope is the STEVEDORE'S KNOT (Fig. 11b). The bulkiness of these three knots can be increased by passing the end through the bight more than once.

Fig. 10

Fig. 11a

Fig. 11b

4. Securing at a Right Angle

Fig. 12

When a rope is made fast to hold something, the strain will frequently come from a direction at right-angles to the point of attachment, whether this be a wire, post, pole, hook, bollard, rock, ice axe, leg post, bough of a tree or another rope. The simplest 'right-angle' hitch is made by taking the rope round the securing point and making a HALF HITCH on its own standing part (Fig. 12). This is a useful temporary securing if the loose end is held by hand, but for more permanent security a single Half Hitch needs to be backed, perhaps by another Half Hitch or, better, to have taken a full round turn of the securing position first to make a ROUND TURN AND TWO HALF HITCHES (Fig. 13). Seizing the loose end to the standing part (see Fig. 32) greatly increases the hitch's holding power.

Fig. 13

However, all of these last three hitches may jam tightly if subjected to a heavy strain, particularly with a wet rope.

Fig. 14

The FISHERMAN'S (or ANCHOR) BEND (Fig. 14) will not jam. *1.* Take a full round turn loosely. *2.* Make a Half Hitch by passing the end round the standing part and through the round turn. *3.* Back this with another Half Hitch that does not pass through the round turn, and stop the end if desired.

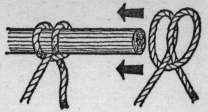

Fig. 15

The Clove Hitch (Fig. 15) is easy to make and particularly useful where you want to keep a long loose end for some other purpose. *1*. Take one round turn on one side of the standing part. *2*. Make a second round turn on the other side. *3*. Tuck the loose end through this second round turn.

Where a securing position has an open end, a Clove Hitch can be made with the end or, usefully, in the middle of a rope by slipping on two loops taken in opposite directions, as in Figure 15. With practice this can be done very quickly. The Clove Hitch unties easily and holds securely, although it may slip under a steady rotating pull.

Fig. 16

A variation on the Clove Hitch is the Miller's Knot (or Constrictor Knot). In this, the loose end, instead of being tucked through the second round turn, is tucked through the *first* (Fig. 16). This takes a little longer but it gives a knot that holds like a boa constrictor on cylindrical surfaces. Very useful for tying the neck of a sack or for holding two pieces of wood together while the glue dries, it is less effective on flat surfaces or corners. When tying a sack, you can fashion the knot ready, then hold the sack's neck with one hand whilst you slip on the knot with the other. *1*. With your length of securing cord make a loose Overhand Knot. *2*. Shift the two ends across to make three loops as in Figure 17. *3*. Slip the middle loop over the neck of the sack and haul tight by the ends. This knot can be difficult to untie and, if you use it, you must be prepared to cut it loose.

Fig. 17

A variation on the Miller's Knot is the OSSEL KNOT. *1*. Take *two* round turns on either side of the standing part. *2*. Pass the loose end through the first turn taken. If this first turn was taken over your thumb as well, a gap for the end will have been left.

The LARK'S HEAD or COW HITCH is a very simple hitch taken with the middle of a line where the strain will come equally on both parts. *1*. Pass a bight of cord round the securing position. *2*. Pass both ends through this bight and pull taut. An alternative to stage *2* is to slip a toggle (see Figure 22b) over both sides of the bight but under the standing part (Fig. 18b). This can be quickly done, will hold well under strain, and can be quickly released simply by knocking out the toggle.

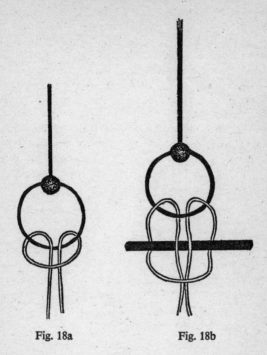

Fig. 18a   Fig. 18b

5. 'Parallel' Hitches

Sometimes a rope has to be made fast to an object that lies roughly parallel to the direction from which the strain will come, e.g. in suspending something from a stay; in lowering a pipe; in hauling a wire. The best general-purpose hitch here is a ROLLING HITCH (Fig. 19). Make this like a Clove Hitch but take *two* turns on that side of the standing part from which the strain will come (e.g. on the lower side when suspending a weight, but on the upper when hoisting a pipe). Then cross the end over the standing part to make the final Half Hitch. For added safety (certainly with synthetic rope) seize the end to the standing part. Always put a Rolling Hitch on a rope *against the lay*.

Fig. 19

To make a Stopper Hitch, start a Rolling Hitch but instead of a final Half Hitch, dog the end round the rope *with the lay* and hold it either with a seizing or by hand. This makes a quick temporary stopper on a rope to take the strain off whilst its end is being moved to a new position or taken to a winch barrel (Fig. 20).

Fig. 20

Timber (or Log) Hitch, used for towing or hoisting a spar or plank, is a Half Hitch taken with a rather long loose end which is then dogged back round itself *with the lay* (Fig. 21). Haul on the standing part to tighten the hitch. To keep the end of the timber pointing in the same direction as the hauling line, slip on another Half Hitch as shown in Figure 21.

Fig. 21

6. *Miscellaneous Knots*

A SHEEPSHANK is used to shorten a rope temporarily or to by-pass a weak section in it. *1.* Gather the amount desired, including the weak section if any, as in Figure 22a. *2.* With the standing parts slip Half Hitches over either end of the loop as in Figure 22b. *3.* For added security, either seize the bights left protruding (right-hand end of Figure 22c) or toggle them (left-hand end of 22c).

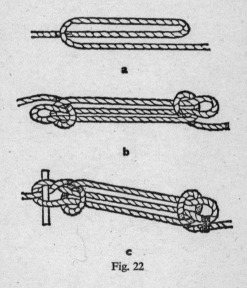

a

b

c

Fig. 22

Use a MARLINE HITCH to lash up long bundles or bend a sail to a spar (see Figures 23 and 74). *1.* Make an eye in the end of a rope (any small loop will do – see Chapter Five). *2.* Pass the other end of the rope round the bundle, through the eye and haul taut. *3.* Continue along the bundle with a series of Half Hitches, keeping them in line and hauling each taut as made. *4.* Finish with a Clove Hitch.

Use a MARLINE SPIKE HITCH to obtain a better purchase or grip on a small cord. *1.* Make an Overhand Knot. *2.* Pass a spike, screwdriver, bolt, etc. through the knot as shown

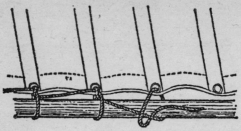

Fig. 23

in Figure 24. *3*. Pull on both ends of the spike simultaneously to tighten.

Many hitches can be fashioned for quick release by taking the last turn with the bight of the rope (i.e. the rope doubled)

Fig. 24

to make a bow. This is what we do in tying shoe laces. Bows, however, may slip; but one that should not – there are others – is the DRAW HITCH *1*. Take one bight of rope up behind the securing position and another in front of it. *2*. Pass the front bight through the back bight and pull taut with the loose end, which leaves the front bight still standing (Fig. 25b). *3*. Make a third bight with the loose end and pass it through the still-standing front bight. Pull taut with the standing part (Fig. 25c). To free, pull on the loose end.

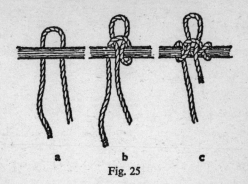

Fig. 25

A ROADMENDER'S KNOT is useful for tying a line along a
row of posts or stanchions and can be made with the middle
of a rope. *1.* Take a turn round the post with a long bight of
rope, passing below both standing part and loose end
(Fig. 26a). *2.* Pass the bight over the top of the post and pull
tight with either the standing part or loose end (Fig. 26b).

Fig. 26

If a line has to be thrown any distance, it needs a weight
at the end to make it carry. You can just tie it round a rock,
but a neater and more permanent way is to make a
MONKEY'S FIST. *1.* Make a hank of three or four turns near
the end of the rope but leaving enough end for succeeding
operations. *2.* Pass the loose end round the waist of this hank
three times. *3.* Pass the end through the loops and round the
turns three times (Fig. 27a). *4.* Complete stages *2* and *3*
twice more. *5.* Work the knot tight. *6.* Either cut off the end

close to the knot (Fig. 27b) or splice the end into the standing part.

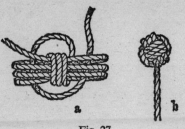

Fig. 27

MOUSING A HOOK is a sensible precaution to prevent the load from jumping out and should be used wherever possible. Simply middle a length of twine on the shank of the hook and take the opposite ends round shank and bill a number of times, finishing with a Reef Knot. This closes the jaw of the hook.

CHAPTER FOUR

JOINING KNOTS (BENDS)

The REEF KNOT is an excellent knot for joining two ends of the same rope *round* something, such as a bundle or the bunched canvas of a reefed sail, but it should not be used as a bend joining two separate ropes, for when not under strain it will loosen and may slip. To make a Reef Knot: *1.* Bring the two ends together from opposite directions and half-knot them, i.e. twist each round the other once. *2.* Bring the ends back and half-knot them again. If, for the first half-knot, you took the right-hand end over the left-hand, for the second take the left hand over the right hand (or if first left-over-right, now right-over-left). With the knot completed, the two parts of each end should lie together side by side in the bight of the other end (Fig. 28a). If one part is above and the other below the bight, you have tied a less secure GRANNY KNOT.

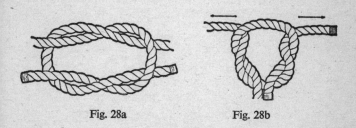

Fig. 28a   Fig. 28b

A Reef Knot unties very easily: jerk one end sharply towards the other and the knot will collapse into an easily opened Cow Hitch (Fig. 28b).

A much safer knot for tying two ropes together is the SHEET BEND (known also as the WEAVER'S KNOT by weavers, the NETTING KNOT by net-makers and probably other names by other trades). It can be used to join two ropes of equal

Fig. 29

size, two of unequal size and one rope to the cringle in the corner of a sail or to an eye. To make it: *1.* Form a bight in the end of one rope (the larger, if of unequal size) or use the eye if there is one. *2.* Pass the other (smaller) rope's end up through this bight (or eye). *3.* With this end take a complete turn round the bight or eye and then pass it under its own part (Fig. 29). With synthetic ropes and wet natural fibre ropes, repeat stage *3* to make a DOUBLE SHEET BEND. If one rope is considerably larger than the other, or if in any doubt, seize the end of the heavier rope to its own standing part to make a temporary eye, or use a HEAVING LINE BEND as shown in Figure 30.

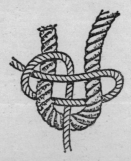

Fig. 30

A bend that is safe and, being flat, does not impede the progress of a rope round a winch barrel is the CARRICK BEND. It is particularly useful for large ropes, especially if

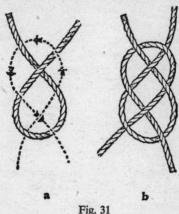

a   **b**

Fig. 31

they are of unequal size. *1*. Form the basic loop with the larger rope (Fig. 31a). *2*. Pass the end of the smaller rope under this loop. *3*. Take this end as shown in Figure 31b *over* the larger rope's standing part, *under* its loose end, *over* one side of its bight, *under* the smaller rope's own part, and *over* the other side of the bight. Note that this makes a symmetrically woven pattern. When tightened, the ends should come out on opposite sides of the knot and each should be stopped to its standing part.

Fig. 32

Most of the securing knots in Chapter Three and the loops in Chapter Five can be used to join two lines if the end of each is taken as a knot round the standing part of the other.

and with synthetic ropes this may be desirable as the two knots jam against each other. Figure 32 shows TWO HALF HITCHES WITH THE ENDS STOPPED BACK. If possible, the 'stopping' cord should be of the same material as the ropes. This is a useful bend with large ropes but with smaller, and certainly with very thin lines such as cottons and fishing lines, a sound and quickly made bend is the FISHERMAN'S KNOT (Fig. 33). With each line, make an Overhand Knot round the other.

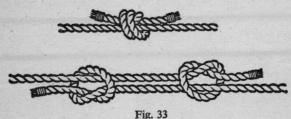

Fig. 33

One point to remember when deciding which bend to use is that some knots, e.g. the Overhand, can be difficult to untie after strain. Twines, cottons, monofilaments and other thin lines are relatively cheap and it will not matter greatly if you simply cut the knots off after use, but you will not want to treat larger, more expensive ropes this way. Remember, too, that knots weaken a rope, and deform it, especially if the rope is synthetic, so it is advisable, other considerations apart, to use those bends that involve the minimum amount of bending and are easy to untie. In this respect, the Two Half Hitches with the ends stopped back have much to commend them.

Situations can occur where you will want to knot two ropes together but are unable to get enough slack to do so because their other ends are secured elsewhere. The knot to use in these circumstances is the SHROUD KNOT. Its making is described in Chapter Six.

CHAPTER FIVE

LOOPS AND NOOSES

1. Loops

The standard loop at the end of a rope, proven throughout centuries of use, is the BOWLINE. *1.* Place the loose end from left to right across the standing part, leaving a loop of the desired size. *2.* Pinch the end and standing part together with the fingertips of the right hand and twist downwards to the right for half a turn. This will bring the end poking up through a small loop (Fig. 34b). (You can, of course, make this small loop first and poke the end up through it, but the other way, with practice, is vastly quicker.) *3.* Pass the end behind the standing part and down through the small loop again (sometimes described as 'putting the rabbit back in his hole') (Fig. 34a). *4.* Hold the loose end and the right-hand side of the large loop together and pull taut.

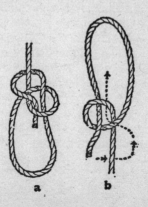

a   b

Fig. 34

With synthetic ropes, it may be safer to stop the end to this right-hand side of the loop below the knot, whilst climbers using Nylon rope should tie a Tarbuck Knot instead of a Bowline (see Chapter Thirteen).

One way of making *two* loops at the end of a rope is to tie a FRENCH or PORTUGUESE BOWLINE (Fig. 35). *1.* Start as for a simple Bowline stages *1 and 2*. *2.* Instead of passing the end round behind the standing part, take it right round in front in a second loop. *3.* Complete as for stages *3* and *4* in a Bowline.

Fig. 35

If you have fallen into water and someone has thrown you a line, you will want to tie a loop round yourself. A MIDSHIPMAN'S HITCH is probably the only knot you will be able to manage (Fig. 36). *1.* Pass the line round your chest. *2.* Pass the end round the standing part and make a Half Hitch inside the loop towards your body. *3.* Then either hold the end tightly against the standing part, or, if you have the time and strength, dog it round the standing part two, three, or four times before holding both tightly together. Now shout to your rescuer to start hauling.

A number of loop-making knots use the rope doubled into a bight. The bigger the bight, the larger the loop will be. If the end of the rope is doubled, the loop will be at the end; but the doubling can be done anywhere along a rope where a loop is needed. One of the soundest, and easiest to untie

after use, is the BOWLINE ON THE BIGHT. *1.* Make a bight
and, using both parts together, follow stages *1* and *2* of a
simple Bowline (Fig. 37a). *2.* Firmly holding the smaller
loop formed where the two parts cross, bring the projecting
bight through it and down towards you and then up behind
the knot to the position shown in Figure 37b. *3.* Haul both

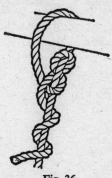

Fig. 36

parts taut together. This leaves *two* loops. They can be left
as they are or worked to different sizes (to fit, for instance,

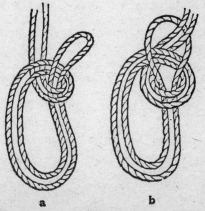

a   b

Fig. 37

one round the chest, the other under the thighs of a person to be hoisted or lowered), by the two long standing parts of equal length, assuming the knot has been made in the middle of the rope. Alternatively, one loop can be worked up to nothing, leaving just a single loop. This is worth considering when needing a loop in a synthetic rope.

Both the Overhand Knot and the Figure-of-Eight Knot, tied with the bight, form secure loops which, however, can be difficult to untie (Figs. 38a and 38b respectively) although this matters less with twines, cottons and fishing lines where the knot can be cut off without great financial sacrifice.

Fig. 38a

Fig. 38b

The MAN HARNESS HITCH provides a way of making loops along a rope, the number depending upon how many people are to be harnessed to whatever it is that has to be hauled. (Because of its frequent use at one time in the hauling of guns it is also called the ARTILLERYMAN'S HITCH.) *1.* Make a loop of the required size as in Figure 39. *2.* Pass the bight 'A' up between 'B' and 'C'. *3.* Bring 'D' and 'E' together and haul taut with 'A'. This hitch could be used for a middleman's loop on a climbing rope but there are preferable knots (see Chapter Thirteen).

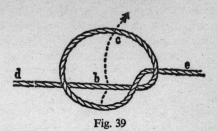

Fig. 39

2. Nooses

A noose is a loop that tightens when under strain. Any loop at one end of a rope can be made into a noose by passing the other end of the rope through it, but easier than that is to make an OVERHAND NOOSE (the HONDA of the South American gauchos). With the end, tie an Overhand Knot *round* the standing part (Fig. 40). This makes the noose, but it is safer to tie another Overhand Knot in the loose end as a stopper.

Fig. 40

An Overhand Noose may prove difficult to untie but a RUNNING BOWLINE will not. *1.* Take the end one full turn round the standing part *2.* Make a Bowline with the end on itself. (Figure 41 does not show stages *3* and *4* of the Bowline.)

Fig. 41

To make a HANGMAN'S NOOSE: *1.* Make a loop with a long loose end. *2.* Double the end back towards the loop. *3.* Bind the end seven or eight times round both the standing part and both parts of the doubled-back end until only a small bight of the latter is left protruding. *4.* Pass the end through this bight and work taut by pulling on the loop.

CHAPTER SIX

KNOTS WITH A ROPE'S OWN STRANDS

A CROWN KNOT binds together the strands at a rope's end and is the first step towards a Back Splice (see next chapter). *1.* Unlay the rope. *2.* Bend Strand I into a bight towards the centre of the rope. *3.* Bend Strand II into a similar bight with its end passing through the bight of Strand I (Fig. 42). *4.* Pass Strand III through the bight of Strand II and work all taut. The Strands come out at the bottom of the knot.

Fig. 42

In a WALL KNOT the strands come out at the top of the knot. *1.* Unlay the rope. *2.* Pass Strand I outside Strand II but inside Strand III (Fig. 43a). *3.* Pass II outside III and the end of I (Fig. 43b). *4.* Dip III outside the bight of II and bring it through the bight of I (Fig. 43c). *5.* Work all taut, cut off the end and whip or fuse (Fig. 43d).

Both these knots can be doubled in size by 'following round', i.e. tucking each strand through the knot again, following alongside, but not on top of, its original lead.

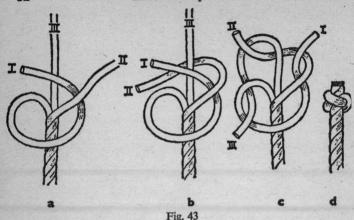

Fig. 43

A marline spike may be found handy for loosening the tucks without untying the knot.

A MANROPE KNOT is a smart, effective stopper at the end of, say, a gangway rope. *1*. Form a Wall Knot. *2*. Form a Crown Knot on top of the Wall (Fig. 44a). *3*. Follow round first the Wall, then the Crown. *4*. Cut the ends off close (Fig. 44b).

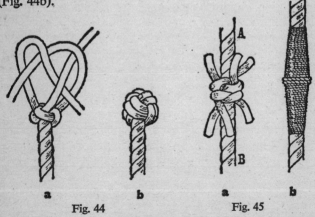

Fig. 44   Fig. 45

A SHROUD KNOT is used to join two ropes (see Chapter Four). *1*. Unlay both ropes and crutch the strands, i.e. pass each strand between two strands of the other rope in the opposite direction to them. *2.* With the strands of rope 'A' form a Wall Knot on 'B' (to the right if using left-handed rope). *3.* With the strands of 'B' form a Wall on 'A'. *4.* Tighten until the knots jam against each other (Fig. 45a). *5.* To make a neat finish, marl and serve (Fig. 45b).

To make a STOPPER KNOT: *1.* Form a Wall but do not work taut. *2.* Pass each end from left to right up through the loop next to it and under the end already there (Fig. 46). Work taut. *3.* Lay up the strands hard, whip and cut off to the whipping.

Fig. 46

A SINGLE MATTHEW WALKER KNOT is a variation on the Wall Knot. *1.* Start like a Wall but pass Strand I under both II and III. *2.* Pass II under III and I and come up through the bight of I. *3.* Pass II round the end of I, through its bight and through the bight of II (Fig. 47).

Fig. 47

A DOUBLE MATTHEW WALKER (Fig. 48a) will not slip or capsize. Each strand passes through *three* bights, including its own (Fig. 48b).

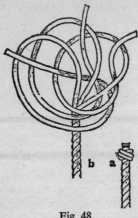

Fig. 48

A DIAMOND KNOT is often made in the middle of a rope, or it can be made round the middle by tucking two lengths of cord through the rope under adjoining strands. If using the rope's own strands, unlay to the desired position of the knot, taking care to preserve the natural lay as you will have to relay later. *1.* Lay each strand alongside the rope so that you leave a bight standing above the point where the strands fork or the cords emerge from the rope. *2.* Take Strand I outside II and up through the bight of III. *3.* (With three strands) take II outside III and up through the bight of I; (with four cord parts, or four strands in a four-stranded rope) take II outside III and up through the bight of IV. *4.* (With three strands) take III outside I and up through II (Fig. 49), work taut and relay rope; (with four parts or strands) take III outside IV and up through I and then, *5.* Take IV outside I and up through II and work taut.

To form a DOUBLE DIAMOND KNOT follow each strand round once. Like the Diamond, the Wall, Crown and Matthew Walker can all be made with four- or six-stranded rope by applying the basic principle of each knot.

A CHEQUER KNOT cannot be made with three-stranded rope but is very suitable for the ends of braided ropes, e.g. bell lanyards. *1.* Unlay to a reasonable length and whip (you will need longer ends than for the knots already described). *2.* In the centre of the fork place a core of some material,

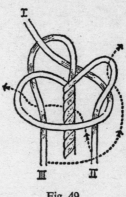

Fig. 49

e.g. a small ball of spunyarn. *3.* Make a Crown Knot left-handed over the core with the even-numbered strands. *4.* Make a Crown right-handed with the odd-numbered strands in such a way that they interlace with the even-numbered (Fig. 50a). *5.* With all strands make a Wall Knot (Fig. 50b). *6.* Follow round Crowns and Wall. *7.* Make a

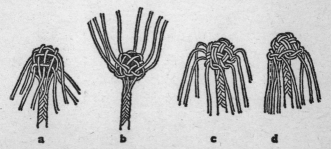

a   b   c   d

Fig. 50

Wall round the bottom of the knot (Fig. 50c). *8.* Make a Crown similarly (Fig. 50d). *9.* Follow round both knots to make a *Turk's Head*. Tuck each strand away under a strand just above the whipping and cut off.

To fashion a TURK'S HEAD on the end of a rope make a Manrope Knot and follow the ends round a second time or more often. To make one on the noose of a whistle or knife lanyard, unlay the end of the lanyard and with the strands form a Wall Knot round the standing part of the lanyard itself. Then form a Crown Knot, also around the lanyard, and follow both round at least twice. This knot will slide up and down the lanyard. To make one that will not, before starting the Wall Knot as above tuck one strand through the standing part.

CHAPTER SEVEN

Splicing is a method of joining one rope to another or two parts of the same rope by tucking the strands of one under and over those of the other. Except in braid-on-braid rope (see next chapter) it reduces the strength of a rope by about one-eighth.

All splices start by unlaying the rope(s) for a certain distance. The point where the unlaying ends is called the 'fork' and here a temporary whipping will prevent further, undesired, unlaying. It may also help, with larger natural fibre ropes, to whip the end of each unlaid strand, whilst with synthetic ropes not only should this certainly be done, but one or two further whippings at different places should be put on each strand to preserve the manufactured lay.

All tucks should be made, unless otherwise directed, *with the lay of the rope* into which they are being made and *at right-angles to it.* The strands can be lifted to allow tucks to be made under them by inserting a metal marline spike or a wooden fid with the lay of the rope. Tucks should be pulled tight along the lay and can be made to lie snugly, which is essential for strength, by stretching and twisting the splice; by rolling it on a table with the palm of the hand or on the floor or deck with the foot; or by hammering home lightly with a wooden mallet. Any splice will look neater and gain in strength if whipped after completion, and with synthetic ropes this is a must.

1. Eye Splices

An EYE, so-called from its shape, is a loop usually, but not always, at the end of a rope. It may be *hard,* if made round

a metal stiffener called a thimble, or *soft* without a thimble.
The most common types of thimble are the HEART THIMBLE,
known from its shape (Fig. 51); the LANYARD THIMBLE,
similar but with a flattened top to allow for more turns of
rope (Fig. 52); and the circular SAIL THIMBLE (Fig. 53).

Fig. 51   **Fig. 52**   **Fig. 53**

To make an EYE SPLICE ROUND A THIMBLE: *1.* Unlay the
rope for a distance equal to three times its circumference
for natural fibre ropes or six times for synthetic ropes.
2. Bend the still-laid-up end round the thimble so that the
fork just reaches the standing part, with the middle and left-
hand unlaid strands on top of the latter (Fig. 54a). *3.* Lightly
stop the thimble to the crown of the eye (and on both sides
of the fork with synthetic rope). *4.* Tuck the middle unlaid
strand from right to left under the strand on which it rests
(Fig. 54b). *5.* Tuck the left-hand unlaid strand from right
to left over the strand under which the first tuck was made
and under the next one (Fig. 54c). *6.* Turn the rope over to
the left so that the right-hand unlaid strand is now on top
of it. *7.* Tuck this strand from right to left under the only
strand remaining under which a tuck has not already been
made (Fig. 54d). This completes the first set of tucks, which
should be worked tight. *8.* With natural fibre rope, tuck each
strand *twice* more, over and under the strands of the other
rope; with synthetic rope complete *four* more sets of tucks
(five in all).

To finish off the splice: either (a) divide the yarns/fila-
ments of each strand into two and whip together adjacent
halves from neighbouring strands (three pairs, all told), or
fuse them in synthetic rope; or, better (b), halve the thick-

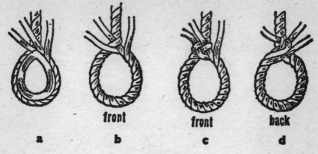

Fig. 54

ness of each strand by scraping and make a complete set of 'half-tucks'; then halve again to make 'quarter-tucks' and halve again to make 'eighth-tucks'. The additional eighths are necessary in synthetic ropes. Finally, with natural fibre ropes, serve over the whole splice from the throat of the thimble downwards, or with synthetic ropes put on a palm-and-needle whipping similarly.

To make a SIMPLE SOFT EYE: as above, but without the thimble.

To make an EYE SPLICE WITH FOUR-STRANDED ROPE: Proceed as for a three-stranded rope but in stage *5* the left-hand strand is tucked under the same strand as the middle one (or rather, the left-hand one of the middle pair) but comes out from under the strand beyond it, i.e. it passes under *two* strands. All four strands must, of course, be tucked to complete the first set.

To make an EYE IN THE MIDDLE OF A ROPE: *1.* Cut the rope where the splice is required. *2.* Splice end 'A' into 'B', tucking as for an Eye Splice. *3.* Splice 'B' into 'A' similarly (Fig. 55). This makes a CUT SPLICE, which can also be used to join two ropes together, though leaving a rather large lump.

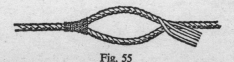

Fig. 55

To make an EYE ON THE SIDE OF A ROPE: *1.* Grip the rope with both hands and twist in opposite directions to force out the strands doubled as in Figure 56, until they are long enough to be tucked for an Eye Splice.

Fig. 56

This last splice is not as strong as a simple Eye Splice. Other splices that should not be subjected to heavy strain but which have certain features that may be desirable in particular situations are:

A SAILMAKER'S EYE SPLICE: Proceed as for a simple Eye Splice but tuck from *left to right*, i.e. against the lay. This gives a neater finish.

An EYE SPLICE WORMED AND COLLARED: Carry out stages *1* to *7* of a simple Eye Splice but then – *8.* Separate four yarns/filaments from each strand. *9.* Keeping these out of the way, complete a normal Eye Splice with the remaining parts of the strands but adding an extra half-tuck. *10.* Lay up the separated yarns/filaments into two-yarn/filament nettles, making three pairs with three-stranded and four pairs with four-stranded rope. *11.* With one nettle from each pair, worm to the end of the splice and finish by tucking each nettle under a different strand. *12.* There are now two sets of nettles, one at the top, the other at the bottom of the splice. With each fashion a Double Diamond Knot round the rope (Fig. 57). This gives a 'fancy' finish to the splice.

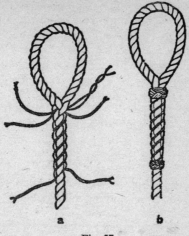

Fig. 57

A FLEMISH EYE: *1*. Unlay one strand to a distance equal to one and a half times the circumference of the desired *eye*. *2*. With Strands II and III form the eye as in Figure 58. *3*. Lay Strand I back into the hollow from which it came but

Fig. 58

in the opposite direction. *4.* Unlay Strands II and III. *5.* Scrape all strands down to taper and marl or serve to the standing part. This makes a useful loop in the end of a large rope for hauling it about.

A SINGLE TUCK EYE SPLICE AND WALL KNOT: After only one set of tucks, make a Double Wall Knot with the strands round the rope. This is useful where the end of a rope has to run right up to a block or pulley because it takes up less space and cannot jam in the sheave.

2. Joining Two Ropes

SHORT SPLICING. A Short Splice is the easiest way of splicing two ropes but is bulky and not suitable for a rope that has to pass through a block or narrow opening. *1.* Unlay both ropes to a distance equal to twice their circumference (natural fibre rope) or three times (synthetic rope). *2.* Crutch the strands together so that each passes between two strands of the other rope in the opposite direction (Fig. 59a). *3.* Put a stop round the fork of 'A'. *4.* Tuck each strand of rope 'A' over the strand of 'B' immediately to its left (looking towards the end of the strand) and under the strand beyond, as in eye-splicing. *5.* Tuck the strands of 'A' again, over and under. *6.* Cut off the stop on 'A' and tuck the strands of 'B' twice into 'A' (Figure 59b, to make the operation easier to follow, shows only one set of tucks on each rope). *7.* With synthetic ropes, make an extra set of tucks on each rope. *8.* Stretch the splice by pulling and twisting. *9.* Either (a) whip or fuse the ends and cut off or (b) put in a set of half-tucks before finishing as for an Eye Splice or (c) take a few of the yarn filaments from each strand to fill up the lay of the rope by worming, scrape down the remainders of the ends, marl them down with thin twine, and serve over the splice.

Two four-stranded ropes are spliced exactly as two three-stranded, but if a three-stranded has to be spliced to a four-stranded: *1.* Unlay the three-stranded rope for twice the distance of the four-stranded, split one of its strands into two equal parts and relay it as a four-stranded rope for the distance needed to take the tucks of the other rope. *2.* Crutch the strands and proceed as above.

Long Splicing. A Long Splice does not produce a bump and can be used on a rope that has to reeve through a block or pulley, but it is weaker than a Short Splice and uses considerably more rope. *1.* Unlay both ropes to ten times their

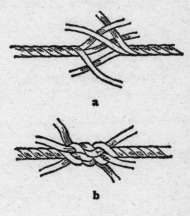

a

b

Fig. 59

circumference (fifteen for synthetic ropes). *2.* Crutch the strands. *3.* Further unlay one strand of 'A' and lay up in its place the opposing strand of 'B' until only some 5 cm (natural fibre) or 10 cm (synthetic) of the 'B' strand remain. *4.* Similarly unlay one strand of 'B' and lay up the corresponding strand of 'A' in its place. *5.* Leave the two remaining strands, one on each rope, as they are (Fig. 60). *6.* Finish off in one of these ways: (a) half-knot each pair of opposing strands, taper the ends and tuck as for a Short Splice; or (b) tuck the tapered ends as for a Sailmaker's Eye Splice so that each end goes continually round the same strand; or (c) as for (b) but before tucking the ends, halve each one and tuck each half round a different strand to that encircled by its 'twin', which gives a very smooth finish.

To long-splice four-stranded ropes, proceed as above but ensure that the four points where the opposing strands meet are evenly spaced. Do not have two close together.

To long-splice a three-stranded into a four-stranded rope: *1.* Unlay both ropes and crutch the strands. (One pair of the four-strands will pass between two of the three-strands together.) *2.* Further unlay one strand of the three-stranded rope and lay in one of the 'four' strands. *3.* Further unlay one of the 'four' strands and lay in one of the 'three' so that the two 'four' strands left are the pair that were crutched

Fig. 60

together. *4.* Divide the remaining 'three' strand into two unequal parts, a third and two-thirds. *5.* Half-knot the 'third' with one of the 'twin' four-strands. *6.* Further unlay the other twinned 'four' strand and lay up the 'two-thirds' in its place. *7.* Half-knot all ends and finish as for a simple Long Splice.

A MARINER'S SPLICE is used to join two cable-laid ropes. Probably you will never need it in earnest but if you want to test your ability, try to make one for if you succeed you will have passed one of the old tests of skill. *1.* Unlay the ends of the cables to six times their circumference. *2.* Unlay each of the ropes of which the cables are composed. *3.* Crutch the strands of each rope with those of the corresponding rope in the other cable in such a fay that the three forks do not come opposite each other. *4.* Long-splice each pair of ropes into each other as described above.

3. Other Splices

A CHAIN SPLICE is used to join a rope to a chain whose link sizes are too small to allow the whole rope to be passed through and brought back to form an eye. *1.* Unlay the rope for about six (natural fibre) or nine (synthetic) times its circumference. *2.* Further unlay Strand I for a distance equal to the circumference of the eye required plus one more complete turn round the rope. *3.* Pass Strands II and III through the end link of the chain and bring them back to form the eye with their still-laid-up parts. *4.* Lay up Strand II into the space left by the extra turn unlaid of I. *5.* Further unlay Strand I for about 30 cm (or 45 cm for synthetic rope) and lay II up in its place. *6.* Half-knot Strands I and II and tuck their ends as for a Long Splice. *7.* Tuck Strand III as for a simple Eye Splice. Figure 61 shows I and II knotted and the first tuck of III.

Fig. 61

A BACK SPLICE, sometimes called 'a lazy man's whipping', stops the end of a rope from unravelling, but it thickens the end, making it difficult to reeve through a block. *1.* Unlay the rope for three times its own circumference. *2.* With the strands, form a Crown Knot. *3.* Tuck the strands back along the rope as for a Short Splice (Fig. 62).

Fig. 62

To work a CRINGLE into a ROPE OR SAIL. A Cringle is a small becket or loop (see Figure 63a). *1.* Take a strand of rope three and a half times the length of becket required. *2.* Tuck one end, tapered, three times into the main rope. *3.* Tuck the other end through the rope so as to leave a loop of the size required. *4.* Dog this working end back round the loop, keeping the turns in the natural lay of the strand. *5.* Pass the working end through the main rope where the first tuck of the standing end was made. *6.* Dog the end back along the loop, filling up all the spaces still left in the lay (so that, in effect, you have laid up a short section of three-stranded rope). *7.* Finish by tucking the working end, tapered, three times into the main rope (Figure 63a shows only one tuck made).

To work a cringle on to the boltrope of a sail, proceed as above but pass the ends through the eyelet holes in the sail instead of the rope and finish by tucking them round the cringle itself (Fig. 63b) until they cross under its crown where they should be cut off.

A TAIL SPLICE joins a fibre rope on to the 'tail' of a steel-wire rope, e.g. to put a pliable securing end on to a wire

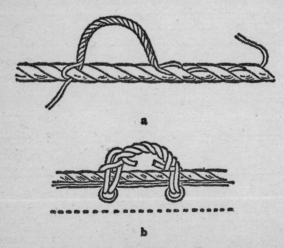

a

b

Fig. 63

halyard. With a natural fibre rope, proceed as for a Short Splice, working the six strands of the wire rope in three pairs. Make at least six tucks on either side of the crutching point and marl, parcel and serve over the whole splice when complete. With synthetic rope this is not too secure a splice (except with braid-on-braid – see next chapter) but if you do make one with such rope, make at least *nine* tucks per side and put on two palm-and-needle whippings, one at either end of the splice, before marling, serving and splicing.

With four-stranded rope, work the six strands of the wire rope as two pairs and two singles.

CHAPTER EIGHT

SPLICING BRAIDED ROPE

Splicing simple braided rope (as opposed to braid-on-braid) is a difficult task because of the tightness of the braiding and might, perhaps, be better left to an expert. If, however, you decide to tackle it yourself, to make a Short Splice, proceed as follows: *1.* Unlay both ropes for a sufficient distance and put whippings on the forks. *2.* Rebraid both ropes more loosely than they originally were as described under 'Round Sennit' in Chapter Fifteen. *3.* Short-splice as for hawser-laid rope but allowing for the differences in the numbers and arrangements in the strands.

Making an eye at the end of a braided rope is somewhat easier for, as with a Flemish Eye, no tucking is involved. Simply unlay the strands for a sufficient distance, form the still-unlaid end into an eye and marl the unlaid strands down to the standing part.

A much neater, stronger job, however, is achieved by using a spindle to make a SPINDLE EYE. *1.* Take a cylindrical piece of wood or metal – the spindle – whose diameter is slightly larger than that of the required eye, and on it raise two lumps with spunyarn about the diameter of the rope apart and half its diameter high (Fig. 64a). *2.* Lay four pieces of seaming twine along the spindle and stop them as shown in Figure 64a. *3.* Unlay the rope, open the strands and separate each yarn/filament. *4.* Knot the yarns in pairs, one from either side, over the spindle between the lumps – which prevent them from spreading out – until all have been used, varying the position of the knots so that they do not all come together, which would raise a bump on the eye (Fig. 64b). *5.* Lay the ends of the yarns/filaments along the standing part and lightly stop them to it. *6.* Cut the stoppers holding the seaming twine and bring its ends together to reef-knot them in pairs tightly over the knotted yarns. 7. Take off one spunyarn lump and slide the eye off the spindle. 8. Staring at the top, serve the eye down to the fork. 9. Take the stoppers off the yarns and scrape the latter down to taper. 10. Serve them down to the standing part. (Not essential, but to give a better finish, cover the eye with cockscombing – see Chapter Fifteen.)

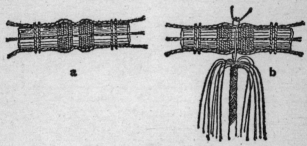

Fig. 64

Braid-on-Braid

A splice in braid-on-braid causes no loss of strength in a rope. The tools needed to make one are a hollow-ended fid and a pusher. Both must be of the correct size for the rope and are obtainable from chandlers. Adhesive tape and a felt-tip pen or other marker are also necessary.

TO MAKE A STANDARD EYE (Fig. 65)
Stage 1 (a) Tape end of rope with one layer of tape.

(b) From this measure one fid length along the rope and mark. This is point 'R'.

(c) Form loop of size required – round the thimble if this is to be included – and opposite 'R' mark a second point 'X'. This is where the core will be extracted.

(d) Tie slip knot five fid lengths from 'X'.

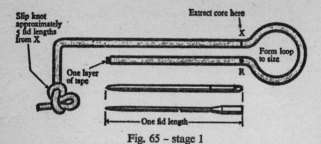

Fig. 65 – stage 1

Stage 2 (a) Bend the rope sharply at 'X'.

(b) With a spike open sheath yarns until sufficient core is exposed.

(c) Pry core from sheath and then pull out completely from 'X' to end of rope.

(d) Put one layer of tape on end of core.

(e) Holding exposed core, slide sheath as far as it will go towards slip knot and then smooth away from knot towards taped end until all slackness is removed.

(f) Tape core where it emerges from sheath (Mark I).

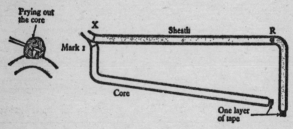

Fig. 65 – stage 2

Stage 3 (a) Slide sheath towards slip knot to expose more core.

(b) From Mark I measure along core towards 'X' one short fid length (this is the distance from the hollow end of the fid to the two marks round it). Make *two* heavy parallel marks on core (Mark II).

(c) From Mark II measure in same direction one full and one short fid length and mark with *three* heavy parallel marks (Mark III).

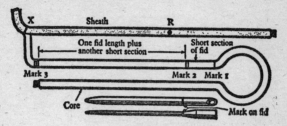

Fig. 65 – stage 3

Stage 4 (a) From 'R' towards the taped end of the sheath count seven consecutive strands going round the rope from either the right or left.

(b) At this seventh strand mark right round the sheath point 'T'.

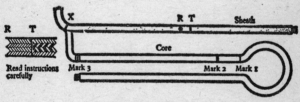

Fig. 65 – stage 4

Stage 5 (a) Insert fid into core at Mark II and slide through and out at Mark III.

(b) Pinch taped end of sheath and jam into hollow end of fid.

(c) Hold core lightly at Mark III and, with pusher point in the taped end of the sheath, push fid and sheath through Mark II to emerge at Mark III.

(d) Remove fid from sheath and pull sheath until 'T' on the sheath meets Mark II.

(e) Remove tape from end of sheath.

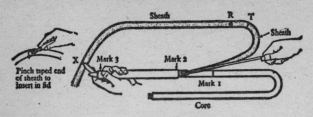

Fig. 65 – stage 5

Stage 6 (a) Insert fid at 'T' on sheath and jam taped end of core in hollow end.

(b) Push fid and core through sheath to emerge at 'X'. If the fid is not long enough to reach 'X', penetrate sheath at some intermediate point, pull through the core and re-insert fid at penetration point to reach 'X'.

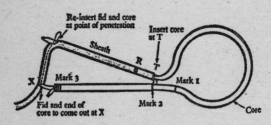

Fig. 65 – stage 6

Stage 7 (a) Lightly hold core at Mark III and pull on sheath tail until core bunches tightly against the cross-over. This exposes more sheath to be tapered.

(b) Remove tape and unlay sheath braid as shown in inset.

(c) Cut groups of strands at staggered intervals to form a tapered end.

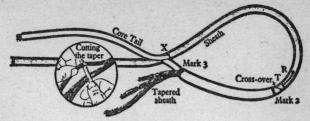

Fig. 65 – stage 7

Stage 8 (a) Bring cross-over up tight by pulling on core tail at 'X', then on tapered sheath at Mark III.

(b) Holding cross-over tightly, smooth out all excess braid away from cross-over towards 'X', then towards Mark III. Tapered sheath will disappear at Mark III. *Do not cut off core tail.*

(c) Hold rope at slip knot. With other hand 'milk' sheath towards splice, gently at first, then more firmly, so that it slides over Marks III and II, cross-over point and 'R'. If bunching occurs at cross-over, tug core tail firmly until bunching disappears, then smooth loop from 'T' to 'X'. Continue until all slackness between slip knot and loop has been removed.

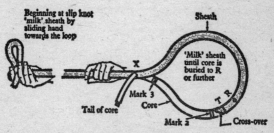

Fig. 65 – stage 8

Stage 9 (a) Put needle and palm whipping on splice as near 'X' as possible, using a fine cord of same material as rope.

(b) If eye is correct for size, cut off core tail at 'X'. If not, recheck Stages *1* to *8* before cutting off. A hollow flat section at the throat indicates that the core has been cut off too short but this does not affect the strength of the splice.

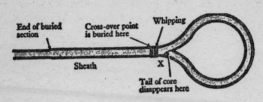

Fig. 65 – stage 9

SPLICING WITH USED ROPE

1. Soak rope in water for a few minutes to loosen fibres.
2. In Stage 2 thoroughly loosen three or four strands to make a large, flexible hole for extracting the core at 'X'.
3. Before burying sheath in Stage 6:
    (a) Anchor loop of slip knot to a firm object and use both hands and weight of body to bury sheath over core at crossover.
    (b) Holding cross-over tightly, 'milk' all excess sheath from 'R' to 'X'. Cut off core tail at 'X'.
    (c) Pull above cross-over with one hand to reduce diameter of cross-over and core, then 'milk' sheath with other hand.
4. Flex and loosen the rope at the cross-over point during the final burying process.
5. Tie a small cord in a Rolling Hitch round the sheath and pull on it towards the eye to remove all sheath slackness during the final burying process.

MAKING A SLING

1. Measure out the length of rope required: for a continuous loop, plus four fid lengths; for an eye at each end, plus five fid lengths.
2. Splice each end of the rope into the other as for a Stan-

dard Eye, when making a continuous loop; or splice a Standard Eye at each end.

MAKING A CENTRE EYE SPLICE (Fig. 66)

1. Measure circumference of eye (including thimble, if required) and mark rope accordingly.
2. Pass end 'A' through Mark II and end 'B' through Mark I, as close together as possible.
3. Insert the thimble, if necessary, and pull taut.

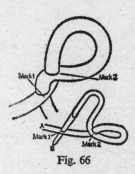

Fig. 66

MAKING A TAPERED SHEET

For best results the smaller rope should be nearly equivalent to the size of the core of the larger, e.g. 8 mm to 10 mm; 6 mm to 8 mm; 5 mm to 6 mm. With a carefully executed splice, the new sheet will have the breaking strength of the thinner rope.

1. Tie a knot in the larger rope roughly two metres from the end.
2. Work the end of this rope to separate core and sheath and slide sheath back towards the knot, exposing the core.
3. Cut off a length of core equal to eight times the circumference of the larger rope, e.g. 25 cm with a 10 mm rope; 20 cm with an 8 mm; 15 cm with a 6 mm.
4. Put a palm and needle whipping on the new core end.
5. Put a similar whipping on the end of the thin rope.

6. Butt the two whipped ends and overstitch all the way round and across both.

7. Smooth the sheath slack away from the knot to bury the core join.

8. Put a palm and needle whipping over the end of the sheath on to the thin rope, tapering the sheath as the whipping proceeds.

MAKING A TAIL SPLICE TO A WIRE ROPE (Fig. 67)

A relevant example of where this splice will be useful is in making a fibre securing 'tail' to a wire halyard. The tools needed are a sharp knife, adhesive tape and a hollow (or Swedish) fid. A splicing fid may be helpful in pushing the wire into the core but is not essential.

Stage 1 (a) Knot the rope to a solid object roughly 10 metres from its end.

Fig. 67 – stage 1

(b) Tape the wire at its end and about 40 cm back. (This is the length to be buried.)

(c) Lightly bind the rope 2.5 cm from its end, fray out its strands and separate those of the core from those of the sheath.

(d) Slide back the sheath to expose about 1 metre of core.

Stage 2 Bury the wire in the core until the latter's rope ends overlap the marker tape by some 5 to 10 cm.

Fig. 67 – stage 2

Stage 3 (a) Tape the core tightly to the wire about 15 cm from the wire marker.
(b) Unlay the core strands back to this tape.

Fig. 67 – stage 3

Stage 4   Neatly divide the core strands into three and bind each.

Fig. 67 – stage 4

Stage 5   Pass the Swedish fid under *two* wire strands.

Fig. 67 – stage 5

Stage 6 Tuck the first rope strands through this, making sure they lie flat and neat.

Fig. 67 – stage 6

Stage 7 Tuck the next rope strands under the next two wire strands.

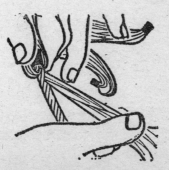

Fig. 67 – stage 7

Stage 8 Tuck the last rope strands under the last two wire strands.

Fig. 67 – stage 8

Stage 9 Complete three full sets of tucks and cut off ends.

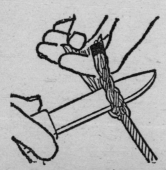

Fig. 67 – stage 9a

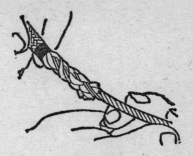

Fig. 67 – stage 9b

Stage 10 Smooth the sheath back over the splice until all slack is removed. Take care not to ruck the core over the wire.

Fig. 67 – stage 10

Stage 11 (a) Tightly bind the sheath where the core splice finishes.

(b) Unlay sheath strands back to this point.

(c) Tuck sheath strands as for core strands in Stages 4 to 9.

Fig. 67 – stage 11(a) (b) (c)

(d) Add one extra half-tuck (see previous Chapter).

(e) If desired, bind the tucks with waterproof tape.

Fig. 67 – stage 11(d) (e)

CHAPTER NINE

SLINGS AND SLINGING

SLING is a general term for any rope taken round an object so as to leave a loop into which lifting gear may be hooked. In climbing (see Chapter Thirteen) a sling is always a continuous loop but the slings used by seamen, stevedores, engineers and others are not necessarily such loops. However, a BALE SLING, whose use on both cylindrical and square loads is seen in Figures 68F and G and 69, is a large continuous loop made by short-splicing the ends of a rope, although reef-knotting or sheet-bending would serve temporarily. Using a Bale Sling as shown in Figure 69 gives the sling four 'parts' or 'legs'. For safe working, the angles

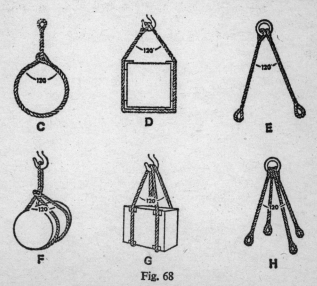

Fig. 68

between neighbouring legs should not exceed 120°. If the cylindrical object is a cask with a bung, and especially if it contains liquid, the parts of the sling should cross in line with the bung so that it is on the upper side while being hoisted.

A single line with an eye at each end can be used as shown in Figure 68C provided that the angle does not exceed 120° and only if at least one eye is 'soft', i.e. does not contain a thimble, and only around a soft load such as a laden sack, for if used on, say, a metal drum, the load could slip.

Fig. 69   Fig. 70

To hoist a cask, barrel, butt, drum or other cylindrical object using only a single length of rope it is best to use a BUTT SLING, a rope with one end fused, whipped or pointed and the other spliced into an eye (or, temporarily, tied into a small Bowline). To use a Butt Sling: *1*. Place the cylinder on its side (bung up, if it is a cask). *2*. Reeve the end of the rope through the eye and slip the loop thus formed over one end of the cylinder. Haul well taut. *3*. Take the end round the other end of the cylinder and clove-hitch it on to its own part, in line with the eye (and the bung, if there is one). Figure 70 shows how this is done, but the sling used should, for safety, be longer.

To sling a cylinder in an upright position, e.g. a drum without a lid, use a single piece of strong rope. *1*. Lay the rope down and stand the drum, open end up, fairly centred on its middle. *2*. Bring the rope's ends up and half-knot them on top of the drum. *3*. Open this half-knot out sideways and work the bights thus formed down one either side of the drum. *4.* Reef-knot or sheet-bend the ends together to make a loop for the hook (Fig. 71).

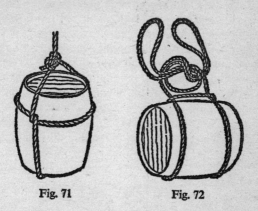

Fig. 71   Fig. 72

NORMAL SAFE WORKING LOAD (SWL). As a general rule, if a sling holds a load by only one or two parts of rope (Figs. 68C, D and E), divide the breaking strength by 12 for synthetic and 8 for natural-fibre ropes; if by four parts (Figs. 68F, G and H) by 6 for all ropes to obtain the SWL. If the angle between parts exceeds 120°, divide by twice the figures given. Knots reduce a sling's strength by up to 50%. Take this into account if you SHORTEN A BALE SLING to a

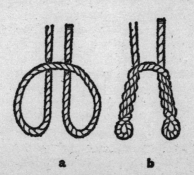

a   b

Fig. 73

required length either by: (a) throwing back a bight and twisting it in two bights to make a catspaw (Fig. 73); or (b) by dividing the large bight into two and half- or reef-knotting the smaller bights (Figure 72 shows them half-knotted). Either way, hook into both the small bights left protruding.

A STROP, to a sailor, is a continuous loop smaller than a sling (although to climbers they are all slings). A SELVAGEE STROP is made from yarns or monofilaments (Fig. 74). *1.* Drive two large nails into a plank at a distance apart equal to the length of strop required. *2.* Secure one end of a ball of yarns or monofilaments to one nail. *3.* Pass turns round the nails until the strop is the desired thickness,

Fig. 74

taking care to pull each turn tight as made. *4.* Bind the strop together with a Marline Hitch, using line twice as thick (and of the same material) as the strop. This makes a pliable strop for securing the hooks of tackles, etc., where no other suitable attachment presents itself, e.g. on a mast, wire, pole, etc. Middle the strop on the mast, etc., and wrap the ends round opposite ways, passing one bight through the other each time they meet. (Figure 75 shows only one turn taken.) To finish, hook into both bights together, or one with a very strong strop.

A GROMMET (or deck quoit) is a small, firm, continuous loop, too small to be short-spliced. *1.* Unlay a single strand of rope to $3\frac{1}{2}$ times the circumference of the grommet required, preserving the natural turns of the lay of the strand. *2.* Close up the middle of the strand into a ring of the size required (Fig. 76b). *3.* Pass the ends round in the original lay until all spaces have been filled (Fig. 76a). *4.* Finish off as for Short Splice (see Chapter Seven).

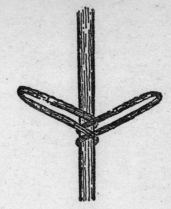

Fig. 75

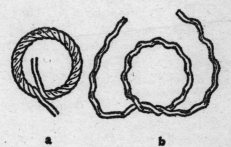

a   b

Fig. 76

When hoisting or lowering a cylindrical object with no crane or tackle available, a PARBUCKLE may be useful (Fig. 77). *1*. Middle a long rope round a post or a bollard at the top of the hoist. *2*. Take both ends under the barrel, etc., and bring them back to the top of the hoist where they are to be held by hand. *3*. Now either haul on the ends (to hoist) or pay them out, taking care to keep an even strain on both parts to prevent the load from slipping out. If a plank can be provided as an inclined plane up or down which the load can roll, this will make the job easier.

A continuous loop can be turned into a carrying sling for

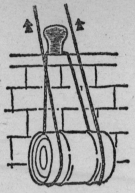

Fig. 77

an object such as a bottle, with a rim or flange at its top, by using a BOTTLE KNOT (also called a JUG SLING and ROPE HANDCUFFS). *1.* Form a loop on the sling as in Figure 78a. *2.* Take the inner left-hand bight *over* the outer left-hand bight; and the inner right-hand bight *under* the outer right-hand. This produces a central loop to slip over the neck of the jug, etc., and two side loops as carrying handles (Fig. 78b). This knot can also be made from a single length of rope by first reef-knotting its end to make a sling.

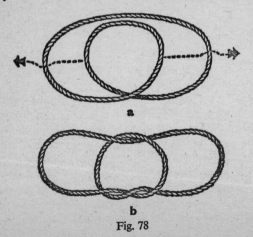

a

b

Fig. 78

THE BAG OR BEGGARMAN'S KNOT, made with a single length of rope, serves the same purpose but more securely and will hold the heaviest, slipperiest bottle, even one with scarcely any rim. *1.* Make two loops in the middle of the rope as in Figure 79a. *2.* Partially cross the right-hand loop in front of the left-hand (Fig. 79b). *3.* Pull the left-hand loop half through the right-hand to make Figure 79c. *4.* Holding the ends I and II firmly with one hand, pass the other hand down through the space 'A' to grip 'B' and pull it through, at the same time allowing the loop 'C' to drop down the back of the knot (Fig. 79d). *5.* Work taut, at the same time working open the central space which will go over the bottle, and knot or splice the loose ends to make a second carrying loop.

Fig. 79

The safest way to sling a plank horizontally to make a stage on which a man can stand is to use a SCAFFOLD HITCH at either end. *1.* Take two turns round the plank, the second being nearer to its end. *2.* Lay the standing part between them (Fig. 80a). *3.* Lift Turn I over the standing part and Turn II and loop it over the end of the plank (Fig. 80b). *4.* Bring the standing part and loose end up and secure with a Bowline. *5.* If using synthetic rope, half-hitch or seize the loose end to itself inside the Bowline as extra protection.

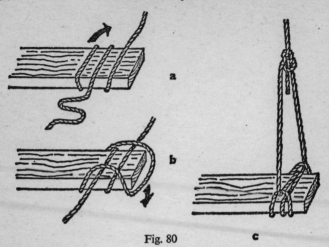

Fig. 80

A Bosun's Chair (Fig. 81) is a cradle in which a man can sit whilst working down a vertical, or near vertical, object such as a mast, flagpole, stay, etc. The seat is made of 25-mm planking about 45 cm by 15 cm. The bridle is a strop drawn through the hole at each corner of the seat before being short-spliced and seized round a thimble. In use, the chair should be held by a lowering-line (called a gantline aboard ship) passing through a pulley or block above, or at the top of, the object to be worked on. The lower end of the gantline may be secured to the ground or deck, or to the chair itself. In the former event, a second person is needed to lower the chair when the man in it wishes to descend even for a short distance, but if the gantline is secured on the chair itself, he can do his own lowering by using a Lowering Hitch.

(Before describing how to make this hitch, a warning: Large-scale cleaning firms use ladders, stage cradles carrying two men, and chairs – which they call Bow Chairs – for individual work in awkward corners. Their employees may opt *not* to work in Bow Chairs or to receive a higher rate of pay if they do. In other words, the work is more dangerous unless considerable care is taken.)

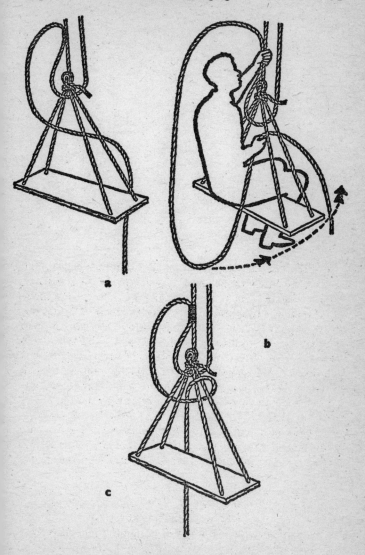

Fig. 81

To make a Lowering Hitch: *1.* Secure the gantline to the chair by means of a Double Sheet Bend with the end stopped securely to the bridle. This is essential whoever is going to do the lowering. The hitch can be seen in Figure 81a. *2.* When hoisted high enough, pass a wracking round *both* parts of the gantline to take the weight whilst the Lowering Hitch is being made (Fig. 81a). *3.* Pull a long bight of loose end of the gantline through the strop, pass it over your head and drop it behind your feet (Fig. 81b). *4.* Pass your feet behind the bight and bring it up in front of you (Fig. 81c). *5.* Haul taut on the gantline and you will find that you have reef-knotted it to the chair, which will hold securely.

To lower yourself: cast off the wracking, pull up some of the slack on the hauling part of the gantline and allow the line to render round, which it will do under your own weight. By keeping the hauling part firmly in hand, you will have the whole operation under control. Nevertheless, it would be as well to practise the hitch and the lowering operation first at a very low level, just in case you make a mistake! Similarly, although experienced riggers dispense with the preliminary wracking and merely hold the two parts of the gantline together by hand whilst making the hitch, do not attempt to emulate them until you, too, are experienced. Remember, too, that in merchant ships, a man is allowed to lower himself only if he is working on the lower-mast. At any level above that a second person must stand-by.

CHAPTER TEN

LASHINGS AND SEIZINGS

1. Lashings

Two spars, e.g. tent poles, masts, scaffolding, sheer legs, trestles, etc. may be fixed together very firmly by a strong rope lashing, the particular method used depending upon the job the spars have to perform. Use:

1. A SQUARE LASHING where the spars under load have a tendency to slide over each other, at the corners in Figure 82.

2. A DIAGONAL LASHING for bracings where the spars may spring away from each other under load, the centre in Figure 82.

3. A SHEER LASHING for sheer legs where the spars have to share a load (Fig. 85) or for joining two spars end to end (Fig. 86).

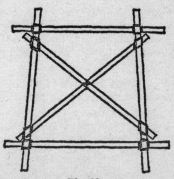

Fig. 82

TO PUT ON A SQUARE LASHING. *1.* Place the spars in position. *2.* Secure one end of the lashing by a Clove Hitch to the spar nearest to the vertical. Make the hitch below the point where the other spar crosses, and dog the loose end round the standing part (Fig. 83a). *3.* Take turns under and over the 'horizontal' spar, behind the 'vertical' spar and over and under the 'horizontal' as in Figure 83b, making some three or four turns and hauling each taut as made. *4.* Put on three or four *frapping* turns *between* the spars as in Figure 83c, pulling each very taut and, if need be, beating them into position. These turns ensure that those of stage *2* will hold the spars tightly together. *5.* Finish with a Clove Hitch on the 'horizontal' spar.

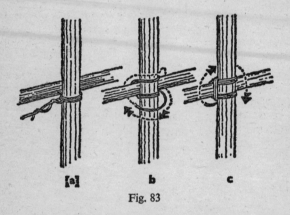

[a]   b   c

Fig. 83

To PUT ON A DIAGONAL LASHING. This should not be put on until the ends of the spars concerned have been securely fixed.

1. Put a Timber Hitch diagonally over the crossing (Fig. 84a). *2.* Continue with three or four tight turns in the same direction as the hitch and the same number at right angles to it (Fig. 84b). *3.* Put on frapping turns between the spars. *4.* Finish with a Clove Hitch over one spar.

To PUT ON A SHEER LASHING. *1.* Start with the legs parallel to each other. *2.* Put a Clove Hitch round one spar and dog the loose end round the standing part (Fig. 85a). *3.* Take a number of turns around both spars together (ten will generally be enough) hauling each taut as made (Fig.

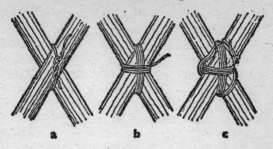

Fig. 84

85a). *4.* Splay out the legs to the required angle without allowing the tension on the lashing to ease and put on three or four frapping turns (Fig. 85b). *5.* Finish with a Clove Hitch on one spar.

When lashing two poles end to end, carry out stages *1* to *3* as above but begin and end with a Clove Hitch round *both* poles and double the number of turns taken. There will be no room for frapping turns so drive in wedges of wood to tighten the lashing (Fig. 86).

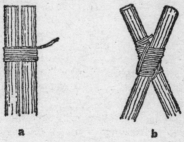

Fig. 85

2. *Seizings*

Seizing is a method of binding two ropes together, or two parts of the same rope, by means of strong, small cord where a splice is not practicable. To be effective, the cord must be bound on very tightly, so if difficulty is experienced in gripping small cord firmly enough, use a Marline-Spike Hitch.

The first step in any seizing is to bring the two ropes together as closely as possible. If, because they are already tautly stretched, this proves difficult, make use of a SPANISH WINDLASS: *1.* Lay a bar horizontally across in front of the ropes. *2.* With the middle of a length of strong twine take a full turn round the ropes. *3.* Dog each end of twine back

Fig. 86

round its own part to form a small eye and with these dogged ends take turns round the bar. *4.* Insert a marline spike in each 'dogged' eye and lever them round the bar until the ropes are tightly together (Fig. 87). Greasing the middle of the twine will allow it to slide more easily round both ropes and bar.

The type of seizing to use depends upon the nature of the strain on the ropes.

A FLAT SEIZING should be used only where the strain upon the ropes is both *equal and light.* *1.* Make a small eye or loop in the end of the seizing cord. *2.* Take a turn with the end of the cord round both ropes, pass it through the eye and haul taut. *3.* Take as many more turns as are required (at least seven) round both ropes, heaving each taut as made. *4.* Pass the end of the cord down *inside* the turns *between* the ropes and bring it through the eye at the other end of the seizing (Fig. 88). *5.* Take one complete frapping turn round the seizing lengthwise between the ropes. *6.* Take two more frapping turns in such a way that they

Fig. 87

make a Clove Hitch. *7.* Work an Overhand Knot tight up against the Clove Hitch as a stopper and cut off. (A Crown or Wall Knot instead of an Overhand will look neater.)

A Round Seizing should be used where the strain upon both ropes is *equal and heavy. 1.* Begin as for a Flat Seizing, stages *1* to *4.* The turns so far put on are called 'the lower turns'. *2.* Take the cord in a second layer of turns in such a way that each turn lies in the hollow between two of the lower turns. The 'riding turns' are bound to be one less in

Fig. 88

number than the 'lower turns'. *3.* Tuck the end of the cord under the last of the lower turns and haul taut. *4.* Finish as for a Flat Seizing stages *6* and *7* (Fig. 89).

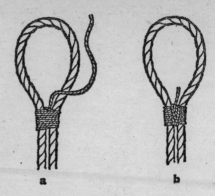

Fig. 89

A RACKING SEIZING should be used where the strain upon the two ropes is *unequal*. *1.* Start as for a Flat Seizing, stages *1* and *2*. *2.* Instead of round turns, dip the end between the ropes and figure-of-eight it round them a dozen or so times. *3.* Dip the end under the last turn taken (Fig. 90a) and haul all the turns taut. *4.* Put on tight round riding turns back towards the eye. *5.* Dip the end between the ropes (Fig. 90b) and finish as for a Flat Seizing.

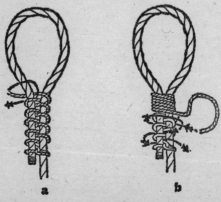

Fig. 90

CHAPTER ELEVEN

BLOCKS AND TACKLES

1. Blocks

THE PARTS OF A BLOCK

The shell is the outside case.

The sheave is the grooved wheel over which the rope travels. If made of lignum vitae, a self-lubricating, very hard wood which makes a fine sheave, it will be scored if used with a wire rope.

The bush is the metal centre of the sheave through which the pin passes.

The sheave pin is the axle on which the sheave revolves, a steel pin that passes through the shell. From time to time it should be punched out with a spike and greased.

The crown is the top of the block, *the tail* is the bottom.

The swallow is the opening between *the cheeks* of the shell (i.e. the sides) through which the rope passes.

The score is a groove on the outside of a wooden block to take a rope strop, and is deeper at the tail than at the crown. Some blocks have two scores to take a double strop. Some, known as *Iron Bound Blocks*, are fitted with a heavy iron strop, whilst an *Internal Iron Bound Block* has a removable forked shaped iron strop down through either side of the shell, often with one fork longer than the other to project as a lug to which the standing end of the tackle may be secured.

Swivel Blocks have a swivel hook or eye at the crown so that they may slew if necessary without twisting the rope.

A Snatch Block has a portion of one cheek cut away and covered with a hinged clamp kept in place with a split pin or spring. This allows the middle of a rope to be placed over the sheave without the necessity of reeving its end through the swallow (Fig. 92).

A Non-toppling Block, used mainly on lifeboat falls, has a tail decidedly heavier than its crown so that it always stays crown upwards. 9 *Tail Block* has a tail of rope instead of an eye, shackle or hook at the crown.

Sister Blocks and *Fiddle Blocks* are double blocks with the sheaves arranged vertically one over the other to save space. In the Fiddle Block one sheave is larger than the other to prevent the rope passing over it from chafing against that passing over its partner.

To FIT A STROP TO A BLOCK: *1.* Make a grommet of rope or wire long enough to pass round the block and the thimble to be secured to its crown (or possibly round a spar to which the block is to be semi-permanently secured). *2.* Worm, parcel and serve the grommet and, to make a first-class job, sew a leather jacket tightly over the serving. *3.* Place the block and thimble inside the strop and secure the whole by both ends, either vertically or horizontally, so that everything is held in position. *4.* Put a tight Round Seizing on the two parts of the strop between the thimble (or spar) and the block (Fig. 91).

Fig. 91

To FIT A DOUBLE STROP TO A BLOCK: *1.* Make a grommet as above but of double the length. *2.* Double it into two equal bights and seize them at the crown. *3.* Carry out stages *3* and *4* above, except that there will be four parts to seize, not two.

2. Tackles

Blocks have two different functions. One is to alter the direction of a rope so that it can be hauled more easily or led to a winch. Almost any block can be so used as a LEADING BLOCK (Fig. 92) but remember that it will have to be fixed by a shackle, hook, knot or splice strong enough to take the strain that will come on it.

Fig. 92

THE LIFTING POWER OF TACKLES

The second function is for blocks to combine with one another to form tackles or purchases which will increase the lifting or hauling power of your arm, capstan, winch, etc. In all tackles except the Single Whip – which offers merely a more convenient hauling position – at least one block moves with the load, and the power ratio of any tackle is the number of parts of rope at this block. Where a rope enters the swallow of a block is counted as one part, where it leaves as another, whilst if the standing end of the rope is secured to the moving block, this also counts as one part.

Types of Purchase

Single Whip : a rope rove through a single final block with one end as the hauling and the other as the loaded part. Power gained: nil. SWL = BS ÷ Z (i.e. *S*afe *W*orking *L*oad equals *B*reaking *S*trength of the rope divided by seven).

Double Whip (Fig. 93): Power gained: double: SWL = BS ÷ 4.

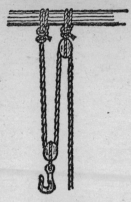

Fig. 93

Gun Tackle : Two single blocks with the standing end of the rope made fast to one. Power gained: double or three times if the standing end block moves. SWL = BS ÷ 4.

Watch or Luff Tackle : A double block and a single to which the standing end is secured. Power gained: three times or four if the double block moves. SWL = BS ÷ 3.

Jigger or Handy Billy (Fig. 94): A Luff Tackle with a tail instead of a hook on the double block. It is often used to obtain greater hauling power on another purchase. Power gained: four times plus the gain already achievable in the other purchase. SWL = BS of tail ÷ 6.

A Runner is a Single Whip with the standing end made fast to a fixed position and the block to another purchase. Power gained: double plus the other purchase. SWL = BS ÷ 7.

A Double Luff Tackle : Two double blocks. Power gained: four or five times dependent upon which block moves. SWL = BS ÷ 2.5.

Three and Two Tackle : A double and a treble block. Power gained: five or six times. SWL = BS ÷ 2.2.

A Threefold Purchase: Two treble blocks. Power gained: six or seven times. SWL = BS ÷ 2.

Tackles larger than a Threefold Purchase are used only on heavy derricks and cranes.

The safety working ratios given above allow for friction in the working parts of the blocks but apply only to the rope used in the tackle. They do not apply to the blocks or pulleys themselves nor to the hooks, shackles, ropes or whatever secures them both to the load itself and to the fixed hoisting position, e.g. a girder, spar, etc. Blocks and pulleys, when acquired, should have a minimum safe working load

Fig. 94

stamped on them, and this should be checked before use. The stress at the load end of the tackle is simply the weight of the load itself but at the standing end it is that weight plus the load on the hauling part. To calculate this it is wise to add 10% for every sheave in the tackle to allow for friction. Thus if an object weighing, say, 140 kg is to be hoisted by a Gun Tackle rigged with the standing part of the rope at the top, then the load equals 140 kg plus twice 10% equals 168 kg. The power gained is double, so the load on the hauling part is 84 kg. Therefore the load on the standing end of the tackle is 140 kg + 84 kg = 224 kg. Allowing a safety factor of six, whatever secures the tackle's standing end must have a minimum breaking strength of 1344 kg. Table I shows that a 1 in (8 mm) hawser-laid Nylon rope will be strong enough but not a $1\frac{1}{2}$ in (12 mm) Grade I manila.

Looking at safety from another angle, 10% can be subtracted from the total load your tackle will bear. The lifting capacity of a Luff Tackle rigged with 1 in Nylon is not 1350 kg × 3 = 4050 kg but that figure less three times 10% which equals 2835 kg. The SWL is therefore 708 kg, which would place a load on the standing end of the tackle of 945 kg.

CHAPTER TWELVE

FOR YACHTSMEN

Various factors such as design, displacement, sail ratio, use and the availability (or non-availability) of finance will influence the choice of ropes, but the recommendations below are a guide towards the most suitable new, top-quality ropes for various purposes. The yacht overall lengths are given in metres and the rope sizes in millimetres of diameter.

Halyards : Use Polyester braid-on-braid or pre-stretched three-strand rope.

Yacht (m)	5	7	10	12	15 and over
Main (mm)	6	8	10	11	12
Jib (mm)	6	8	10	12	12
Spinnaker (mm)	6	8	8	10	12

Sheets: Use Polyester braid-on-braid in larger boats. In dinghies special braid-on-braid or plaited sheets in Polyester, Nylon and Polypropylene are available.

Yacht (m)	5	7	10	12	15 and over
Main or Jib (mm)	10	10	10	12	12
Genoa (mm)	10	10	12	14	16
Spinnaker (mm)	8	10	12	14	16
do. light weather	6	6	8	8	10

Anchor Ropes: Use Nylon, preferably braid-on-braid, with several fathoms of chain at the anchor end to reduce chafe on the sea bottom and keep the anchor stock at the right angle. A chain anchor warp should be three times and a rope warp five times the maximum depth at high tide. As a rough guide the diameter of an anchor rope should be in millimetres 50% more than the overall length of the boat in metres, e.g. overall length 12 metres, diameter of anchor rope 18 to 20 mm.

Mooring Ropes: Again Nylon, either braid-on-braid or three-strand, is best for shock absorption but Polypropylene has the advantages of being not only cheaper but also lighter and buoyant.

Yacht (m)	5	7	10	12	15	17	20
Nylon (mm)	8	12	14	16	18	20	24
Polypropylene (mm)	10	14	16	20	22	24	28

Topping Lifts: Use Polyester, braid-on-braid or pre-stretched.

Ski Tow Ropes: Use 6-mm Polythene or 7-mm Polypropylene.

CHAPTER THIRTEEN

FOR CLIMBERS

1. Ropes

Weight for weight hawser-laid Nylon rope is not as strong as kernmantel (a braided sheath round a core of filaments) but finds favour among climbers because its elasticity – it can stretch over 40% under load – is a considerable asset in countering the shock-loading involved in checking a climber's fall. The Nylon hawsers listed in British Standard 3104:1959 are:

Size No.	Weight per 100 feet	Diameter	Breaking Load
1	1¼ lbs	5 mm	1000 lbs
2	2½ lbs	7 mm	2000 lbs
3	4¼ lbs	10 mm	3500 lbs
4	5½ lbs	11 mm	4200 lbs

A BSI standard rope will bear the maker's name, nominal weight, BS 3104 and the BSI kite mark.

Ken Tarbuck, the mountaineer who invented the Tarbuck Knot, recommends ropes for use as follows:

For rock climbing: No. 4 single or No. 3 doubled.

For Alpine mountaineering not involving extended rock pitches: No. 3 single.

For fixed and running belay slings: the heaviest rope available, preferably No. 4, and protect it where in contact with the rock with a sleeve, preferably of leather.

For Abseil rope: No. 2 or heavier.

For Abseil slings: Rot-proofed manila or Italian hemp (BS 2052) of 6 mm diameter or heavier. *Do not use Nylon* as the friction at a single point in the sling may melt it.

For Abseil sit slings : No. 2 or heavier.

For waist lines : Preferably seven turns of rot-proofed manila or Italian hemp. *Do not use Nylon*; or, if you cannot avoid using it, use a No. 1 rope, clip in a karabiner and make the climbing rope fast to that, which is sound practice even with a natural fibre rope.

Attempts to economize by using lighter ropes than those recommended can be dangerous, for in checking a fall, a thinner rope, even if its breaking strength is adequate, will stretch further than a heavier. This will mean that the falling climber will fall further, thus increasing the risk of injury. A thinner rope is also likely to be proportionately weakened more than a thicker one by abrasion and friction.

Take care of your rope. Always carry it properly coiled when not in use and, when you want to use it, drop the whole coil first to the ground. Then lift off the end on top of the coil and let the rope come naturally as you pull it. This will ensure that it does not kink as it uncoils. As far as possible, avoid treading on your rope, dragging it over rough surfaces, storing it near heat or allowing it to be contaminated by chemicals. Beware, too, of second-hand or borrowed ropes. You don't know where they've been!

2. Knots

The knots described in earlier chapters are largely unsuitable for climbing since they may slip when made in Nylon rope and subjected to the very severe strains that can be placed upon them. Kernmantel, being springier, is even more difficult to knot correctly than Nylon hawser. The knots a climber needs to know – and be able to tie without thinking in the dark with frozen fingers – are:

The WAISTBAND TIE (Fig. 95): This is an ordinary Reef Knot but taken with long ends that are then tucked through the rope.

Fig. 95

The FISHERMAN'S KNOT (see Chapter Four, Figure 33): This joins two rope ends by passing each through an Overhand Knot made in the other. It is suitable for Nylon and may be preferable to the Waistband Tie when using Nylon rope for a waistband.

The BOWLINE (see Chapter Five, Figure 34): Safe with natural fibre ropes but not with Nylon when climbing.

The BOWLINE-ON-THE-BIGHT (see Chapter Five, Figure 40): This will hold in Nylon but is somewhat complicated to tie.

The TARBUCK KNOT: This is tricky to tie and dangerous if incorrectly tied, but properly made it fashions a safe loop for the end man on a rope which can also, when not under strain, be closed by sliding the knot down the standing part. *1.* With a long end, form a loop. *2.* Take *three* full turns with the lay round the standing part *inside* the loop. *3.* Take a fourth full turn with the lay *outside* the loop, coming up on the side of this turn *away* from the loop. *4.* Pass the end down through this turn into the loop and work taut (Fig. 96a). If the loop is to go directly round the climber's body, tuck the end through the standing part inside the loop, i.e. below the knot and some 10 cm from it, to limit any movement of the knot under shock-loading (Fig. 96b). If, however, the loop is to be clipped into a waistband karabiner,

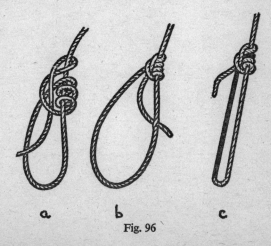

a   b   c

Fig. 96

do not make this tuck. Instead close the loop down on the karabiner by sliding the knot down the standing part (Fig. 96c).

MAKING A SLING: Before setting out for the mountains, slings can be made by short-splicing the two ends of a rope (see Chapter Seven). The splices should be served or given a palm-and-needle whipping and if the sling can be given a tough canvas or leather sleeve for protection against the rock, so much the better. A spliced sling often tends to twist with age.

To make a sling quickly, join the two ends of a suitable length of rope with a Fisherman's Knot (Fig. 97). Alternatively, use a Tarbuck Knot made with one end on to a point near the other end in the reverse direction to that used at the end of a climbing rope. Overhand-knot the unused end

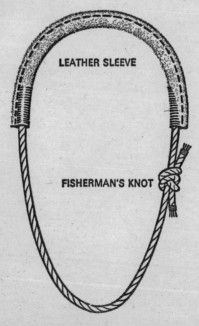

Fig. 97

to ensure that it cannot slide through the Tarbuck. A sling so made can be adjusted in length by sliding the Tarbuck along the rope.

The PRUSIK KNOT (Fig. 98): Invented by the Austrian mountaineer, Dr Prusik, this allows a sling of Nylon rope to be fastened securely to the main climbing rope, either as a loop to go round the middle man's body or be clipped into his karabiner, or to be used as a foothold. It jams tightly under strain, but otherwise can be slid easily up or down the rope (or the rope can be drawn through it), but if a lot of rope is to pass through, it should be slackened off first. To make the knot, pass one end of the sling twice round the rope and then through itself. When using a knotted sling, the knot should be kept clear of the coils.

Fig. 98

The ANCHOR KNOT. A climber may anchor himself by using the climbing rope as shown in Figure 99. *1.* After looping over the anchoring point, bring the rope back to the waist. *2.* Pass a bight up through the waistband and tie a Figure-of-Eight Knot round both the anchoring and active parts of the rope. *3.* Adjust the Tarbuck to the karabiner to make the anchoring parts just taut.

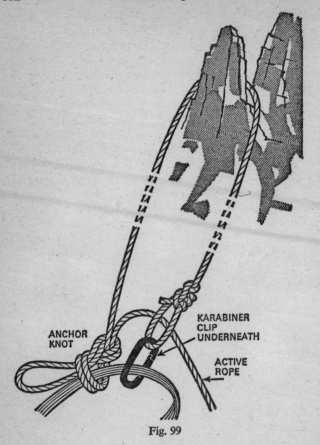

ANCHOR
KNOT

KARABINER
CLIP
UNDERNEATH

ACTIVE
ROPE

Fig. 99

For a climber having the climbing rope looped directly round the body: *1*. As above. *2*. Pass the bight up between the loop and body. *3*. Tie two Half-hitches with the bight round all three ropes or, for the middle man, who will have active ropes to two other climbers, round all four.

LOOPS FOR THE MIDDLE CLIMBER. When a climbing party of three uses two ropes, both will come to the middle climber who should tie on each with a Tarbuck, preferably clipped into two separate waistband karabiners. If only a single rope is used, however, a different loop is needed, as a Tarbuck cannot be tied in the middle of a rope.

A sling secured to the rope by a Prusik Knot will not weaken the main rope and its position can be shifted if circumstances demand. If no sling is available, a loop must be fashioned in the main rope, reducing its strength by up to 25%. The Overhand and Figure-of-Eight Loops (see Chapter Five) taken with a long bight of rope will hold securely but could be difficult to untie later. The Man Harness Hitch (see Chapter Five, Figure 38) can, if pulled severely both ways at once, turn into a constricting noose, so that it could be dangerous to use it round a climber's body. Clipped into a karabiner, however, this possibility would not matter, and the knot would still be relatively easy to untie after use.

CHAPTER FOURTEEN

FOR FISHERMEN

1. Lines

Most anglers use Nylon or Terylene lines, either monofilament or braid. The latter may not shoot so easily but is kinder to the hands and less likely to tangle. A new line should bear the maker's guarantee of its breaking strength, but remember that this is for a new *dry* line. After prolonged immersion, Nylon absorbs up to 11% of its weight in water and can lose 15% of its strength, so that, for instance, a 4.5 kg line at the end of a day's fishing may have a b.s. of only 4 kg. Lines are also weakened by abrasion on faulty rings, rocks, etc. – nicks, such as can arise from entanglement with a hook, are especially weakening – and by exposure to sunlight. Fraying and brittleness are signs of weakness.

To test the breaking strength of a used or otherwise suspect line, suspend from it a bucket which you gradually fill with sand. When the line breaks, the weight of the bucket plus sand will be the line's b.s.

A line should be matched to the rod on which it is used. A light line on a very heavy rod will snap on striking, since the rod will not bend enough to absorb the shock-loading on the line. Alternatively, a light rod will be too 'bendy' if used with a heavy line. When surf-casting, the leader should be not only heavy but also longer than the rod. Using a doubled-line leader by making a long Bimini Twist (see below) is one answer. Another is to tie a shock leader to a smaller Bimini Twist on the reel line using a Surgeon's Knot (see below).

FLY LINES are graded according to Association of Fishing Tackle Manufacturers numbers, based on the weight of the first 9 metres of taper and belly but excluding any parallel tip the line may have.

AFTM Fly Line Classification

AFTM No.	Tolerance in grains
1	54 to 66
2	74 to 86
3	94 to 106
4	114 to 126
5	134 to 146
6	152 to 168
7	177 to 193
8	202 to 218
9	230 to 250
10	270 to 290
11	318 to 342
12	368 to 392

A good fly rod should carry the AFTM No. for which it is designed, although not all fly-line manufacturers are completely accurate about their tolerances.

The angler can make his own tapered leaders if he wishes from lengths of varying thicknesses of Nylon monofilament joined by Blood Knots (see below). A rough guide to the lengths needed is the '60–20–20 Rule', i.e. 60% of heavy mono, 20% of medium and 20% of light; so that a 10-foot leader might have 6 feet of 11-kg line, 2 feet of 5.5 kg and 2 feet of 2.75 kg. These lengths and weights could be broken down into even shorter gradations. The weakest knot in such a sequence is likely to be the last before the fly. If, therefore, the last two sections are joined, not by a Blood Knot, but by interlocking loops (see below) this may give greater strength and will also allow for the rapid interchange of points when fish are rising, if, beforehand, the angler has prepared a number of final tips. To make untreated Nylon sink, coat it with fine mud or with weak detergent and water; to make it float, coat it with a good silicone.

However, the manufacture of tapered fly-lines has reached a level of scientific design and technology that the angler may not be able to match. Good lines are expensive, however, and the angler will generally get the quality he pays for. For the care of specially prepared fly-lines:

DO: stretch the line before use and after prolonged storage;
   use a very light knot, whipping or connector to join leader to line;
   balance line and rod;
   let the line extend fully on the back cast;
   store in a loose coil away from light and heat;
   clean with a cloth moistened in soapy (not detergent) water;
   practise casting on water only.

DON'T: let the line touch detergents, insecticide ointment or spray, line or fly floatants, cleaners or conditioners, oil, grease, petrol;
   let an automatic reel whip the line back through rod rings;
   practise casting on hard surfaces or without a fly or leader;
   crack the line like a whip;
   stamp on a line, catch it in a car door, cut it with a fly, etc;
   pull hard on a line to extricate it from a tree or riverbed.

WIRE – as a monofilament, braided or plastic-coated – is used when hunting large fish whose teeth might sheer through a plastic line. Monofilament wire cannot be knotted. If bent too sharply, it will kink and weaken; but braided wire will bend, although it may not straighten fully afterwards.

2. Knots

Although recent experiments have produced knots that cause little, if any, loss of strength in a line, most knots create some weakness by distorting the molecular structure of a synthetic line. Indeed, some experts recommend that after every trip the last foot or so of the line should be cut off as worthless.

Synthetic lines are springy and 'reluctant' to be knotted. Knots in them should be tightened with a firm steady pull – except some Blood Knots which require a sharp, decisive jerk. Every effort should be made to get a knot right the first time for 'having to have a second go' will usually weaken it. It will always help if, before tightening, the line(s) are moistened with saliva or water. Loose ends should be trimmed close – except where needed for a dropper – with nail clippers, scissors or cutting pliers, whilst a knot that will be repeatedly passing through a guide can be given a streamlined coating of a rubber-based cement to avoid snagging. Wherever possible, tie as many as possible of the knots likely to be needed on a trip before setting out, when the environment will be more conducive to careful, accurate tying than, say, in a bucking boat or a river where the fish are rising all around. The choice of line(s) for any particular trip will depend on various considerations, but as far as knotting is concerned, the easiest monofilament to tie is medium-stiff.

TYING ON TO A SPOOL. A synthetic line bound very tightly on to a spool will damage it. Before winding on, therefore, cover the hub with two or three layers of some natural fibre twine or string, and periodically – and certainly after a 'heavy' battle – strip off the line and rewind. An ultra-light spool should not be loaded with a line above 2 kg b.s. nor a 5-cm diameter hub with one above 4.5 kg b.s.

To tie on: *1*. Take the end of the reel line once round the hub. *2*. Tie an Overhand Knot in the end of the line. *3*. With the end, tie an Overhand Knot round the standing part. This makes an Overhand Noose that will bind tightly on to the natural fibre seating.

MAKING LOOPS. The easiest loop to tie, but with only 75% efficiency in strength, is the DOUBLE OVERHAND LOOP, which can be made anywhere on a line. *1*. Double back the end or take a bight where the loop is required. *2*. With the bight, tie an Overhand Loop (see Figure 38) but take the bight *twice* round and through the knot, not once. *3*. Tighten by pulling on the loop and the standing part. (With this and most other knots, certainly with heavier lines, it may be necessary to protect the hands by gripping through gloves or a rag, or by pliers.)

The BIMINI TWIST is 100% efficient but more complicated to tie and more suitable for larger loops. It should be

tied sitting down. *1.* Double back about 1 metre of the line.
2. Put one hand in the loop and with the other holding the
loose end and standing part together, twist the loop through
20 revolutions. *3.* Slip the loop over both knees together
and keep the twists under tension by holding the standing
part and the loose end at 90° from each other, each 45°
from the vertical (Fig. 100b). *4.* Easing the standing part upwards, pull the loose end down to a 90° angle with the line
of the twists, at the same time slightly spreading the knees.
The loose end will roll down over the top twist. *5.* Spreading
the knees and pulling down and feeding the loose end will
bring the latter rolling down to the fork of the loop (Fig.
100a . *6.* Carefully move the hand holding the standing part
downwards to grip the fork and prevent the twists from
loosening *7.* With the loose end tie a Half Hitch round the
nearer side of the loop and work it up tight. The twists will
now be held. *8.* With the loose end make a Half Hitch round
both parts of the loop but pass the end twice more round
and through the hitch before working tight against the fork.
9. Trim the loose end to 6 mm.

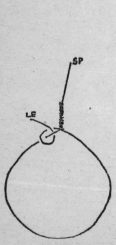

Fig. 100a   Fig. 100b

To make a very long loop, e.g. for use as a double-line, a second person will be needed to hold the loop. A simpler version can be tied by securing the standing part so that one hand can hold the loop whilst the other binds eight turns of loose end round the standing part and then another eight downwards on the first layer. All turns should be tightly taken. Finish with Half Hitches, first on one arm, then on the other of the loop, and trim off.

Another loop comparable to the Overhand is the STANLEY BARNES KNOT, tied like a Figure-of-Eight Loop but with an extra half-turn (Fig. 101).

Fig. 101

To make a loop in monofilament wire, use the HAYWIRE TWIST (Fig. 102). *1*. Make a loop of the required size. *2*. Holding the standing part and loose end in separate hands, twist each round the other to make 'X's' six times. *3*. Take the loose end six times round the standing part in parallel barrel twists. *4*. Rock the end back and forth until it breaks off. Do *not* cut the wire. It would leave a sharp, dangerous projection.

Fig. 102

The HEATED TWIST is a quick, 95–100% efficient way of making a loop in plastic-covered wire. *1*. Make the loop or thread through the eye of the hook, lure, etc. *2*. Twist the loose end and the standing part round each other four times. *3*. Holding them tightly together, warm gently with a match flame about 2.5 cm below them until the plastic coverings have fused; but be careful neither to melt away nor burn the plastic.

JOINING TWO LINES. An easy, efficient way of joining two lines, where acceptable, is to tie them to opposite ends of a swivel. In sea fishing in particular, this has the advantage that rotation caused in one line will not be transmitted to the other. For fly-fishermen, light, specially designed swivels are available (see below).

The standard line-joining knot is the BLOOD KNOT. Each line is taken round the other three, four or five times (Figure 103 shows four) before the ends are passed in opposite directions through the central loop. For full (95%) efficiency, probably five turns are needed with lines of similar, or nearly similar, size. To tighten: with light lines, pull steadily on the standing parts; with heavy lines, jerk decisively.

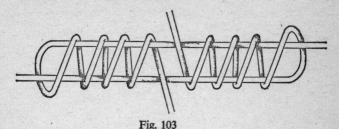

Fig. 103

If the lines are of markedly dissimilar sizes, use an IMPROVED BLOOD KNOT. With this *the light line is doubled* and taken five times round the heavy, but the latter is taken only *three* times round the light. This knot must be jerked just once to tighten. (Efficiency: 90–100%.) If a dropper is needed, use the heavy line end.

The COVE KNOT (or FOUR-TURN WATER KNOT) is an extension of the Fisherman's Knot (see Chapter Four), with high efficiency and good streamlining. With each line make an Overhand Knot round the other but take each end *four* times through its knot, not just once.

The SURGEON'S KNOT is suitable for tying a light line to a heavy, as, for instance, in securing a shock leader. If the light line has already been tied into a Bimini Twist, the efficiency will be almost 100%. *1*. Overlap the outer end of the light reel line and the inner end of the shock leader by about 15 cm. *2*. With the lines side by side, tie an Overhand Knot, taking all the rest of the leader through the knot. The inner end of the leader will finish on the rod side; the outer end of the reel line on the hook side.

INTERLOCKING LOOPS can only be used near the end of a line, as, for instance, in joining leader (cast or trace – the terms vary from place to place) to the reel line. *1*. Make loops in the end of each line if not already there. *2*. Pass the leader's loop over the reel line's and push it up the reel line out of the way. *3*. Pass the other end of the leader through

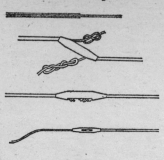

Fig. 104

the reel line loop and pull it down until the loops interlock.

JOINING A FLY LINE TO ITS BACKING. One way is to use SWIVELS as shown in Figure 104. Another is to use a NEEDLE KNOT. *1.* Pierce the butt of the reel line with a needle stouter than the fly line, to emerge about 2.5 cm away (Fig. 105a). *2.* Withdraw the needle and thread the fly line through the hole. *3.* Bind the fly line round the reel line four or five times beyond the exit hole. *4.* Lay the end of the fly line over the exit hole pointing away from the reel line's butt end. *5.* Starting with the furthest-away turn, bring each turn of the fly line back to cover its end and the exit hole, working as tight as possible. *6.* Holding the turns in place with one hand, with the other pull on the standing part of the fly line to tighten. *7.* Varnish over the knot.

An alternative from stage *3* is: *3.* Lay the needle along the reel line with its eye beyond the line's end. *4.* Bind the fly line four or five times round the reel line and needle, covering the exit hole and working *towards* the butt end. *5.* Thread the fly line through the needle eye. *6.* Pull needle and fly line through the whipping to tighten. *7.* Varnish over the knot.

Figure 105b shows another alternative. A short length of 14-kg braided Nylon has been sewn through the reel line by both ends, which are then laid along the line towards its butt. A Needle Whipping (see Chapter Two) is then bound tightly round all parts using fine silk thread and the whole varnished over.

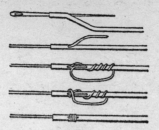

Fig. 105a

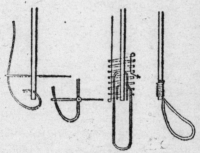

Fig. 105b

TYING TO A HOOK, FLY, LURE OR SWIVEL

The DOMHOF KNOT: *1.* Thread through the eye. *2.* Lay a bight of line along the shank of the hook. *3.* Take the end five times round both parts of the line and the shank. *4.* Dip the end through the bight. *5.* To tighten, grip the loose end and pull on the hook (Fig. 106).

Fig. 106

The IMPROVED CLINCH KNOT (efficiency – 95%): Light monofilament should be doubled before tying this knot. *1*. Thread. *2*. Take five turns round the shaft. *3*. Dip the loose end through the loop between the eye and the first twist. *4*. Pass the end through the loop formed by the loose end and the twisted part. *5*. Pull on the end to tighten (Fig. 107).

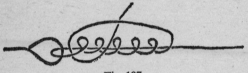

Fig. 107

The 3½-TURN CLINCH KNOT, for use with monofilament of over 27 kg b.s. As for the Improved Clinch Knot but omit stage *4*, and to tighten hold the standing part in a hand protected by a glove or rag and pull on the hook using pliers.

The PALOMAR KNOT (efficiency – 95–100%), for use with light monofilaments. *1*. Double the end and thread with this. *2*. Tie an Overhand Knot with the threaded loop and the standing part. *3*. Slip the loop over the hook. *4*. Pull on the standing part to tighten so that the loop slips past the eye of the hook before jamming (Fig. 108).

Fig. 108

The JANSIK SPECIAL (efficiency – 98–100%) is also suitable for light monofilaments. *1*. Thread through the eye. *2*. Take the loose end *twice more* through the eye to make two parallel loops. *3*. Take the loose end round the standing part and through both loops *three* times. *4*. To tighten: hold the hook with pliers, the standing part with the other hand and the loose end with your teeth before tightening with a steady pull on all parts.

The TWO-CIRCLE TURLE KNOT (efficiency – 88%) is particularly suitable for a fly on a hook with a bent-back eye, as it keeps the alignment of the fly correct. *1*. Thread and push the fly up the line out of the way. *2*. Form the end into two parallel circles. *3*. With the loose end, tie an Overhand Knot round the upper parts of both circles and pull it tight. *4*. Push the loose end and the fly through both circles. *5*. To tighten, pull on the standing part and both circles, closing one after the other, so that they close round the neck of the fly.

The TROLLING SPOON LOOP is for use with solid or plastic-coated wire. Tie the knot like a Palomar but instead of stage *4* wrap the bight of wire all the way round, in and out, of the loop of the Overhand Knot. Then *5*. Barrel-wrap the doubled wire round the standing part. Plastic-coated wire can be Heated-Twisted.

SECURING A WIRE TO A BRAIDED REEL LINE. *1*. Tie a Bimini Twist in the end of the reel line. *2*. Thread the wire up through the loop and take seven turns of wire round both parts of the loop, working away from its bight. *3*. Take seven more turns working towards the bight. *4*. Thread the end of the wire *down* through the remaining bight. *5*. Twist the loose end of wire four times round its standing part and break off. The end might be Heated-Twisted but be careful not to damage the reel line.

SECURING A BRAIDED WIRE TO A HOOK OR LURE (efficiency – 95–100%). *1*. Thread the wire through the eye. *2*. Bring the end back and tie a Figure-of-Eight Knot (see Figure 11a) round the standing part. *3*. Tighten and trim.

A STOP KNOT FOR SLIDING FLOATS. Take a short length of line of the same weight and structure as the reel line. *1*. Lay one end of the length along the reel line roughly where the knot is needed. *2*. With the other end, bind round reel line and length four times. *3*. Dip the working end back through the first turn taken. *4*. Largely tighten knot, slide along line to exact position required, and complete tightening.

The DUNCAN LOOP can be used with artificial lures. It will permit action by the lure but will jam down tightly under pressure from a fish. *1*. Thread through the eye. *2*. Fold back 20 cm of loose end. *3*. Refold about 12.5 cm of this towards the eye to make a second loop. *4*. Take the loose end five times round *both parts of the first loop* but passing always *inside* the second loop. *5*. Pull on the loose end, using fingers, to tighten. Then slide the knot to where it is wanted and further tighten using pliers.

TYING ON TO A SPADE END HOOK (called SNELLING in the USA). *1*. Lay the end of the line along the shank of the hook. *2*. Make three or four turns around both shank and line, working back towards the 'spade'. *3*. Pass the loose end through the first turn taken, between the turn and the shank. *4*. Pull on the loose end to tighten and then, holding the hook with pliers, further tighten by pulling on the hook and the standing part (Fig. 109).

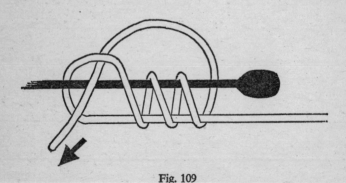

Fig. 109

SPLICING FLY LINES. This is a task probably best left to the expert, but if you wish to attempt it yourself: *1*. From both ends, scrape off 2.5 cm of the plastic or oil dressing.

2. Tease out the braided ends with a needle. *3.* Lay the ends together from opposite directions, smoothing the teased fibres evenly over each other. *4.* Using a fine Nylon thread, put on a Needle Whipping, making at least six stitches through the lines. *5.* Varnish over with a polyvinyl sealer.

SPLICING AN EYE AT THE END OF A FLY LINE. *1.* Scrape off 5 cm of dressing. *2.* Tease out the braided end. *3.* Cut out the core. *4.* Form an eye of the required size by bringing the teased-out fibres back to the standing part. *5.* Smooth the fibres evenly along and around the standing part. *6.* Using a fine Nylon thread, put on a Needle Whipping as above. *7.* Varnish over.

CHAPTER FIFTEEN

MATS, SENNITS, PLAITS AND COVERINGS

1. Mats

A rope mat for the deck or floor will not only be functionally hard-wearing; properly made in clean rope, it can be a delight to the eye.

An OVAL MAT. *1.* Lay the rope as shown in Figure 110a in three loops. *2.* Carry end I over end II, under the bight 'A', over 'B', under 'C', over 'D', under 'E', over 'F', under 'G', over 'H', under itself and over 'A'. This forms Figure 110b. *3.* Now follow round, either taking I back along the path of II or vice versa. This following round may be completed as many times as desired. (Figure 110c shows once only.) *4.* Finish by leaving the ends under strands where they will not be seen.

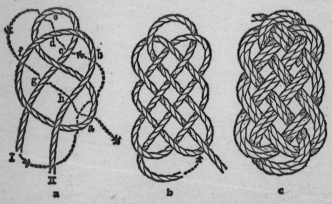

Fig. 110

A SQUARE MAT. *1.* Make the loops as shown in Figure 111a in the middle of the rope. *2.* Pass the bight 'A' over 'B' and under 'C' but do NOT pass 'D' on the other side of the same loop. *3.* Make a loop on end I and pass it under end II (Fig. 111b). *4.* Pass the bight 'E' (but not the bight 'F') over 'D', under 'B', over 'C' and under 'A'. *5.* Form a similar loop on end II (which will now be to the left of I), pass it under I and similarly pass its uppermost bight only through the design alternately over and under crossing strands. *6.* Repeat this operation of passing a loop under one end and a bight up through the design, using the two ends alternately, until the mat has reached the desired size. *7.* Finish by passing an end, which has not been doubled into a loop, to the right under the other end and up through the middle of the design, over and under, until it emerges at the top (Fig. 111c).

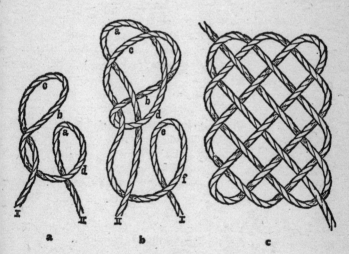

Fig. 111

A CARRICK MAT. *1.* Make two loops as in Figure 112a. *2.* Pass end I over end II, under 'A', over 'B', under 'C' and over 'D' (Fig. 112b). *3.* Follow each end round the other's path once (as in Figure 112c) or more often.

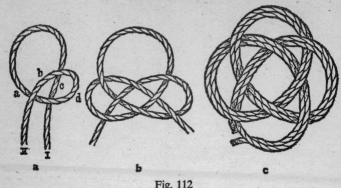

Fig. 112

2. Sennits

SENNIT is a general term for braided ropes, in which the strands are plaited, not twisted, together. The commonest form, used for log lines, sashcord, better quality clothes lines, etc. is ROUND SENNIT, which may be made from any even number of strands, although six or more will look better formed round a heart. The latter, however, has been omitted from Figure 113a for easier illustration. *1.* Whip the ends of the strands together. (It is possible to make a Round Sennit end to a laid rope by dividing the latter's strands into the number required. In this event, put the whipping on the laid rope at the point where the sennit is to begin.) *2.* Cross each neighbouring pair of strands and, allowing the even-numbered to hang down, lift the odd-numbered up out of the way. In Figure 113a the even-numbered strands have gone to the right and the odd-numbered to the left. They will continue to go in the same directions. *3.* Pass each even-numbered strand over the odd-numbered strand *to its right* and when this has been done, hold the former up and allow the latter to drop down (Fig. 113b). *4.* Cross each odd-numbered strand over the even-numbered strand *to its left*, hold it up and allow the even-numbered to drop down. *5.* Repeat stages *3* and *4* alternately and the result should be Figure 113c. The pro-

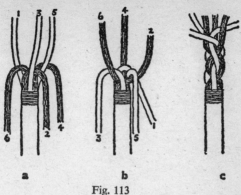

Fig. 113

cess may sound complicated but in practice is very simple.

SQUARE SENNIT is made with eight, twelve or sixteen strands. *1.* Divide the strands into two equal lots. *2.* Take one strand from the right-hand lot and lead it round the back and through the middle of the left-hand group back to its own lot, e.g. with eight strands it will pass outside two and inside two of the left-hand strands (Fig. 114). With twelve, outside three and inside three; and with sixteen, outside four and inside four. *3.* Take a strand of the left-hand lot and pass it round the back and through the middle of the right-hand group to return to its own lot. *4.* Repeat stages *2* and *3* alternately, using each strand in rotation. To begin with the sennit may seem somewhat shapeless, but after a few passes have been made it will tighten up.

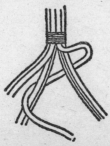

Fig. 114

FLAT SENNIT (Fig. 115). *1.* Secure the strands (any number) over a rope or bar. *2.* Bring the right hand strand across to the left passing it alternately under and over the other strands. *3.* Repeat stage 2, taking care to keep the sennit straight by slanting the other strands to the right.

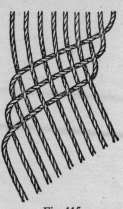

Fig. 115

FRENCH SENNIT (Fig. 116). *1.* Start with an odd number of strands and divide them into two groups, one with one more strand than the other (the right-hand in the illustration).

Fig. 116

2. Work the outside strand of the larger group over and under its companions until it becomes the inside strand of the other group. (It goes from right to left in the illustration.)
3. What was the smaller group is now the larger, so take its outside strand over and under its companions until in its turn it becomes the inside strand of the other group.
4. Repeat stages 2 and 3 alternately.

COMMON SENNIT also requires an odd number of strands.
1. Divide them into two groups, one with one more strand than the other. 2. Bring the outside strand of the larger group across and add it to the smaller (which, of course, now becomes the larger). 3. Repeat stage 2 *ad infinitum.* (Figure 117 shows Common Sennit being made with three strands.)

Fig. 117

3. Plaits

Plaits are allied to, but more complicated than, sennits. They may be made with one strand or with a number. The simplest single-strand plait is the Chain Plait. *1.* At the end of the strand, make an Overhand Knot but use a small bight at the nearby end, instead of both ends. This will leave loop 'A' as in Figure 118a. *2.* Through loop 'A' pull a small bight of the loose end 'B'. *3.* Through the new loop thus formed, pull another bight of the loose end and so on to make Figure 118b. *4.* To finish, run the end through the last loop.

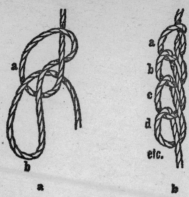

Fig. 118

A DOUBLE CHAIN PLAIT is slightly more complicated. *1.* Form a Figure-of-Eight Knot but do not pull it tight (Fig. 119a). *2.* Dip the end I through the bight 'B'. This leaves a new bight under 'A'. *3.* Dip the end through the new bight. This leaves another new one under 'B'. *4.* Continue dipping the end through each new bight and finish by running the end through the last bight and working taut (Fig. 119b).

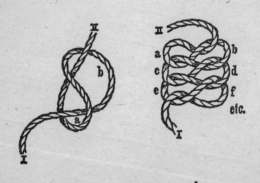

Fig. 119

A SQUARE PLAIT looks like a Square Sennit made with eight strands, but requires only one for its own manufacture. *1.* Make an Overhand Knot with the bight as in Figure 120a. *2.* Pass the end I through the knot to make loop 'B'. *3.* Pass a bight of the end I through loop 'A' to make loop 'C' (Fig. 120b). *4.* Tighten loop 'A' by pulling on the upper side of loop 'B'. *5.* Pass I through loop 'B' to make loop 'D' (as 'C' was made in 'A'). *6.* Tighten loop 'B' by pulling on the upper side of loop 'C'. *7.* Continue passing a bight of the loose end alternately through loops to left and right and drawing the loops tight (Fig. 120c). *8.* To finish: pass the end through the last loop but one made, through the last loop, and down between the last two middle strands and haul taut.

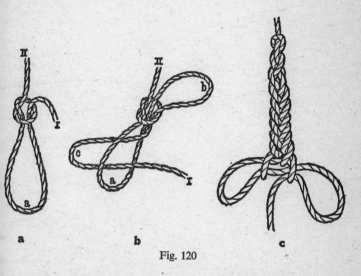

Fig. 120

Plaits can be made with three or more strands by repetition of some of the knots described earlier in this book.

Continuous Crowning, for instance, i.e. Crown Knots fashioned one after the other with the same strands, will produce a plait. If all the Crowns are made in the same direction, a spiral design is achieved; if alternately to right and left, a chain pattern. Continuous Wall Knotting will not produce a satisfactory plait unless made round a heart, but Continuous Walling and Crowning, i.e. Wall and Crown Knots alternating, will. So, too, will Continuous Diamond and Crown Knotting, although this requires greater skill, especially if using a number of strands.

An OVERHAND KNOT PLAIT can be made with four, six or eight strands. Whip the ends of the strands together and number them in a circle. Then Overhand Knot pairs of strands in the following sequences:

With four strands: 1 with 3, 2 with 4, 1 with 3, 2 with 4, etc.

With six strands: 1 with 4, 2 with 5, 3 with 6, etc.

With eight strands: 1 with 4, 5 with 8, 2 with 7, 3 with 6, and so on, retaining the same sequence.

4. Covering a rope

There are two reasons for covering a rope: to protect it and to decorate it. For the former purpose, worming, parcelling and serving provide a general protection against the weather and normal wear and tear. However, occasions arise when a rope – or even more likely a wire – may be rubbing against something softer than itself, in which event it is the latter that requires protection. Sails are, of course, an obvious example.

The best way, generally, to deal with this problem is to bind something relatively soft and yielding round the rope or wire. One material of ancient use for this is BAG O' WRINKLE, which is simply, if somewhat tediously, made. *1.* Seize together the ends of a long piece of small cordage and stretch it out, doubled. *2.* Insert a piece of wood to act as a spreader keeping the two parts away from each other. *3.* Middle a thrum of some soft laid stuff across the two lines and pull its end up between them. *4.* Fill up the length of the lines with thrums so attached (Fig. 121).

COCKSCOMBING can be both decorative and functional, e.g. on the Spindle Eye described in Chapter Eight. With a single line it is simply Half Hitches put on alternately to

Fig. 121

right and left as in Figure 122a. Greater protection and more elaborate decoration are gained by using more strands. *1.* Stopper these to the rope, ring or whatever it is that has to be covered. *2.* With each strand in succession, form two Half Hitches; one towards, one away from the starting point and continue in this way, always taking that strand which is farthest back (Fig. 122b).

POINTING A ROPE has a double purpose, for in addition to being the neatest it is also the soundest way of protecting a rope's end. *1.* Put a stop on the rope at a distance from its end equal to three times its circumference. *2.* Unlay the rope to the stop and then unlay the strands. *3.* Split a number of outside yarns and make an even number of nettles. *4.* Stop

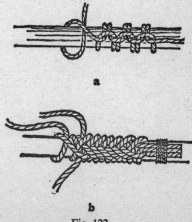

a

b

Fig. 122

these nettles back on the standing part. *5.* Scrape the remaining yarns down to a tapering heart and marl them down very tightly with twine. *6.* Divide the nettles, laying every alternate one along the heart and allowing the others to drop down away from it. *7.* At the point where they divide into those going up and those down, bind on three turns of twine, and take a hitch with the last turn. *8.* Reverse the nettles, i.e. those that were up come down and vice versa. *9.* Take three more turns of twine and hitch (Fig. 123). *10.* Continue repeating stages *6* to *9* until the point has reached the desired length. *11.* Finish off by working a small eye in the end with nettles and yarns marled over with twine.

Fig. 123

The rope need not end in an actual point; it can be a truncated cone, if wished. Moreover, the number and order of nettles taken up or down need not be as described above, which gives merely the simplest design. They can, for instance, be worked in groups of three or four, only one of which is taken up at a time whilst the others are held back, which will produce a spiral effect; and once you have grasped the underlying principles of pointing, there is no reason why you should not devise your own, individual, pattern.

A number of variations can be achieved by working in various fancy knots such as the Turk's Head, Diamond Crown and Wall Knots.

One method of making the point itself which does not employ the rope's own yarns, is to cover the heart with HALF HITCHING. *1.* Stop one end of the twine on the heart. *2.* With the other, make a series of Half Hitches round the last turn of the stopping, as shown in Figure 124. *3.* Put on second, third, fourth rows, etc. to cover the heart making each hitch through the bight of the Half Hitch above it in the preceding row.

Fig. 124

Here again the point may be started with a fancy knot and the first row of Half Hitches made through its lowest turn. If Half Hitching is to look smart, however, it must be tightly made and it may be found that a needle is necessary to pass the end through tautly-hitched bights. The most satisfactory kind to use is a sailmaker's needle with palm.

Half Hitching is also suitable as a decorative – and to some extent protective – covering for bottles, jars and other cylindrical objects. On these it is probably better to start with a decorative knot or a length of tight chain plaiting in order to provide a firm base on which to 'anchor' the first row of hitches.

Another similar and simply made covering is SPANISH HITCHING, suitable for use with small cord, although unlike Half Hitching, it employs a number of separate strands, not one continuous piece. *1*. With the end of one strand – called the warp – middle a number of hitching strands around the rope or other object. *2*. Take the warp round again, a short distance below its first circuit and with each of the hitching strands make a round turn round it. *3*. Repeat stage *2* until the covering has reached the desired length. Various patterns are possible, depending upon the way the round turns are made. In Figure 125 each of the hitching strands has been taken in the following way round the warp: outside, under, behind, over and to the right of its own standing part. They could be taken: behind, under, outside, over and down to the left of the standing part. Numerous other combinations will suggest themselves, but remember that whatever the pattern, it must repeat itself consistently.

Fig. 125

COACH WHIPPING (or CROSS POINTING) makes a very attractive covering with thin or thick strands or with strips of good cloth. It is a favourite design on telescopes, and is suitable for any cylindrical object and for the middle or end of a rope. It requires an even number of strands – like Round Sennit, to which it is related – but these may consist of one, two, three or any number of individual parts. The illustrations show four strands, each doubled in use, which is the maximum that one person can handle easily by himself.

With more than that number, it is better to have an assistant to hold the strands already laid up in place whilst the cross-pointing continues. With six strands the starting sequence would be: 1 over 2; 3 over 4; 5 over 6. With eight it would be the same plus 7 over 8. After that, every strand continues round in the direction in which it is already proceeding, passing alternately over and under its neighbours going the other way.

Thus, starting with four strands numbered in rotation, Figure 126 is obtained by passing: 1 over 2 and 3 over 4; 4 over 1 and 2 over 3; 1 over 2 and 3 over 4. (Now 1 over 2 will complete the beginning of the next sequence.)

Fig. 126

Continuous Crown, Wall and Diamond Knotting can each, individually or in combination with one of the others, be used to cover a rope. Stop the ends of the strands to the rope where the covering is to commence and then make a sequence of the chosen knots.

With the coverings described so far, there is no limit to the distance they may be carried from the starting point, although, of course, one will usually have been chosen beforehand. With the Pineapple Knot and a Herringbone Weave, however, the limits are fixed at the very beginning.

A PINEAPPLE KNOT makes a very attractive raised handle on a rope or covering for a bump such as is formed by a

Shroud Knot or Short Splice. *1.* Provide a smooth covering to the Shroud Knot or, if this is to be merely a handle, raise a 'mouse' on the rope, by winding on marline or yarns. *2.* Stick two pieces of cord long enough to make the knot through the 'mouse' at one end – use a pricker of some sort to do it – at right angles to each other. *3.* Put a light whipping on them and crown them as shown in Figure 127a. *4.* Take the four ends of cord spirally down to the other end of the 'mouse' and whip them temporarily. *5.* Crown the end upwards right-handed (Fig. 127b). *6.* Work the cord back to the top of the 'mouse' by tucking each alternately under and over the strands of the spiral already put on, in the opposite direction to the spiral. You now have two spirals interlocking and the whippings may be cut off. *7.* Follow round until the 'mouse' is closely covered (Fig. 127c). This knot makes a form of cross-pointing and three or more cords can be used if desired.

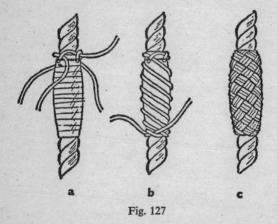

a   b   c

Fig. 127

HERRINGBONE WEAVE. *1.* Lay six or eight long strands along the rope, etc. and seize them at either end of the space to be covered. *2.* Skew them diagonally so that they run at an angle of 45° to the run of the rope. *3.* Tuck the lower ends up and to the right over and under until they reach the rim of the weave. *4.* Tuck the upper ends down and to the left similarly. This will make the right-going diagonals double whilst those to the left have remained single as in Figure 128a. 5. Continue tucking both sets of ends – when at the top, down and to the left; when at the bottom, up and to the right – over and under until the weave is completed as in Figure 128b. 6. To finish off: scatter the ends well, tuck them out of sight after trimming them, cut the seizings and draw out the weave evenly. Variations to the pattern can be achieved by taking ends over two and under two, over two and under three and so on (but be consistent!).

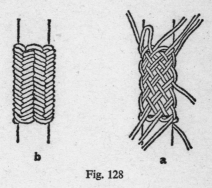

b   a

Fig. 128

PART II
Steel Wire Ropes

CHAPTER SIXTEEN

THE CONSTRUCTION AND CARE OF STEEL WIRE ROPE

1. Types of Wire Rope

Steel wire rope lends itself to specialized constructions designed to meet particular needs.

This book, limited for space, cannot deal with every make of wire rope so below we deal only with ropes likely to be of use in yachting and other recreations and hobbies. These all come into the category known as ROUND STRAND ROPES. They are given this name because they all consist of strands round in cross-section, made up of long threads of steel (wires) which are also round in section. The number of strands is usually six, laid up right-handed round a fibre heart, but exceptions exist where eight strands are twisted round a fibre heart and others where six encircle a core which is, in effect, a smaller wire rope on its own account (Fig. 129a).

The threads which make up the strands of wire rope vary considerably in diameter. The size of a rope is increased without altering the arrangement of its strands by thickening the wires of which they are composed. This, naturally, increases its weight as well as its breaking strength. On the other hand, a rope with a greater number of threads per strand will, in general, be stronger than another of the same size but with a lesser number of threads, without being correspondingly heavier. It will also be more flexible, a quality which is further increased if every strand, as well as the rope itself, is twisted round a fibre heart (Fig. 129b).

Usually the threads have a left-handed twist in contrast to the right-hand run of the strands, and a rope so constructed is said to have an ORDINARY (or REGULAR) LAY;

but sometimes the threads have the same twist as the strands. This construction, known as LANG'S LAY, offers a better wearing surface when in use but should only be installed by an expert, and not employed where there is any danger of the load being allowed to rotate.

The easier wire for a novice to handle is one with a PRE-FORMED or TRUE LAY. In this type the threads and strands are shaped, before laying up, to the helix they will require in the completed rope. This is said to make the rope more resistant to kinking, to give it a longer life, and to place a

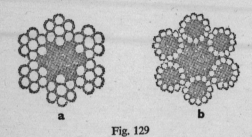

a   **b**

Fig. 129

more balanced load on the strands, but perhaps its greatest attraction is that the strands do not fly apart when cut. In wire rope of normal construction the strands, and the threads within the strands, are like steel spring under tension so that unless the end of the rope is whipped they will separate, often violently. As we shall see in the next chapter, this poses certain problems in splicing which would not be encountered with pre-formed rope.

Further, when a thread in the latter breaks, it lies flat. It neither thrusts into adjacent wires, thus damaging them, nor does it project outward like a needle ready to dig into any unwary hand sliding along the rope. This is a tremendous boon in any wire that is constantly handled, for projecting ends can be extremely dangerous, so much so that it is advisable to wear leather gloves when working with wire of normal lay.

2. Uncoiling and Coiling

It is vital when using wire rope to prevent kinks developing, if only because it is the devil's own job to take them out once they have been formed, although, of course, their effect upon the life and strength of the rope is equally important. Opening a new coil therefore demands the greatest care and a wire rope should always be unwound in the opposite direction to which it was made up.

If the rope is light and flexible, the coil can be rolled open along the ground or deck in the same way that a fireman lays out a hose (Fig. 130).

Fig. 130

If it is too heavy or inflexible for this treatment, it must be held still and rotated as the wire is taken off, always from the outside. (Never start with the inside end.) Just how this is to be done depends upon whether the rope arrives packed in a coil or on a reel. If the latter, pass a shaft through the reel and place it on standards as in Figure 131. Then cut

Fig. 131

the outside lashings only and haul off the rope, applying some form of brake to the reel to ensure that the rope never slackens.

A coil, on the other hand, needs to be lashed down on to some form of turntable with two strong battens secured crosswise on top of it to prevent any turns from springing off and kinking. The turntable, like the reel mentioned above, should be braked to keep the rope tight.

If no turntable is available, lash two substantial pieces of wood together to form a cross and secure two bridles of strong rope to them, with the four ropes' ends each fastened securely to a separate leg about half-way between the end and the centre of the cross. These bridles should be long enough for their bights to reach up through the middle of the coil when it is laid on the cross. Now hook a tackle or crane wire on to the bridle, hoist the coil far enough to allow it to revolve freely, and proceed as for using a turntable (Fig. 132), remembering to keep the wire taut as you haul it off. If the tackle or crane hook is of the swivel variety,

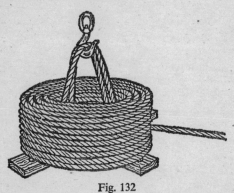

Fig. 132

so much the better, for it will revolve with the coil whilst the crane wire or tackle will remain stationary. If it is not, after every few revolutions the coil must be lowered and unhooked in order to take the turns out of the tackle. A wire rope packed on a reel can also be run off by this method if no shaft or standards are available.

Stowing a wire when you have finished with it is just as important a task to do correctly as breaking open a new coil. If the rope is not too long or large, it may be coiled by hand – in a clockwise direction if it has a right-handed lay, anti-clockwise if left-handed – and the coil should be firmly stopped in at least three places with spunyarn or other small cord in order to prevent the turns springing off. If the rope is large and/or long, it should be wound on to a reel and its outer end lashed down. A wire rope thrown down higgledy-piggledy will almost certainly develop kinks.

Because a wire rope not in use is better kept on a reel, when a length is being taken off a new coil for a particular purpose, measure carefully what you will require and then add on 45 to 60 cm for each splice you intend making. You may, for example, intend putting an eye in one or both ends.

3. Cutting a Wire Rope

Having decided where you want to cut the rope, put a stout yarn whipping on either side of that point. *This is essential* for all wire ropes except for those with a pre-formed lay, for if you do not do it, as soon as you cut through the strands they will fly apart and you will not be able to lay them up properly again.

Scissors and knives are useless for cutting wire ropes; for that task you need a hammer and a cold chisel. To obtain a firm, even cut: lay the rope on some solid foundation of metal or stone (wood is too soft), then flatten the surface between the whippings with a few sharp blows from the edge of the hammer; finally, hammer the chisel through the flattened part.

Lastly, to obtain the longest possible service from your wire ropes oil them occasionally and do not run them through blocks that are too small.

Oiling lubricates and protects the strands. The particular dressing to be applied will depend upon how the rope was treated during manufacture and advice should be sought of the manufacturer or supplier. Galvanized ropes do not need oiling to the same extent as non-galvanized ones, although they will last longer if so treated, but since in a yacht's rigging oiled ropes are likely to leave some most unsightly stains on sails, yachtsmen prefer to rely solely upon the galvanizing to protect the steel wires from the attacks of rain and sea water. The same consideration applies wherever else a wire rope comes into contact with cloth, e.g. in the cord through the top of a tennis net.

However, if the yachtsman lays his boat up for the winter, a thin coating of Vaseline on all his wire ropes will help to lengthen their lives. It can be wiped off easily in the spring. A more permanent alternative is to clean the ropes thoroughly and apply a coating of marine varnish.

A very satisfactory alternative to oiling or galvanizing is the modern plastic covering of wire ropes. Ropes so covered, however, are extremely difficult to splice and if fittings such as eyes are required putting them on is a factory job; the factory will, however, gauge the fitting to the rope, making a seal which will have greater strength than any splice.

Those whose acquaintance with galvanizing is confined to objects such as dustbins, on which the zinc coating is relatively thick, must remember that on steel ropes it is very thin and can easily be knocked off by running the ropes through blocks whose sheaves are either too rough-surfaced or too small. Therefore smooth sheave surfaces with emery paper and always use adequately sized blocks.

CHAPTER SEVENTEEN

1. General Remarks

The tools needed for wire splicing are:
Hammer
Tucker for splicing small strands
Marline-spike, round or with a wedge-shaped point
Cold chisel
Pair of steel wire cutters
Vice
Flat marline-spike
Serving mallet, preferably one with a small reel attached to the handle to hold seizing wire.

This list gives the ideal; the reality often falls short of it; but the hammer, chisel and spike are essential, whilst it is possible to splice only small wires without a vice, and even then the job is easier with one.

One other 'tool' deserves mention although it is, in fact, a substitute for splicing, not an aid to it. This is the WIRE ROPE CLIP. For some reason this is rarely referred to in books on wire splicing, perhaps because its use is frowned upon by purists, but from my experience three such clips will hold two wires together very efficiently. (See Figure 133 for their use in forming an eye.) Their great attraction is that it takes only a few minutes to screw three on with a wrench where a splice might take half an hour or more; their drawback is that they are ugly and cannot be used

Fig. 133

on a wire that has to reeve through a block or pass round a winch drum.

Worming, parcelling and serving are used on wire ropes, and particularly on splices, for the same reasons that they are used on fibres, and they are put on in the same way. However, instead of spunyarn, Seizing Wire is often put on for the serving. This is a very thin, flexible seven-ply, galvanized wire, of six strands twisted round a seventh that forms the heart, made in various sizes from one-sixteenth to one-eighth inches. As well as for serving, it is also used for seizings, such as are described in Chapter 10, or any other form of binding on *wire* rope, but it should not be used on others.

Because seizing wire is small to hold and often greasy, it is sometimes difficult to pull tight. A Marline Hitch should NOT be used to obtain a better purchase as it will probably damage the seizing wire. Instead, lay the handle of a hammer near the head, across the hauling part of the wire, and take a round turn with its loose end between the hammer head and the hauling part. Now hold the loose end against the handle and you can take a good pull without fear of the wire slipping, for the hauling part will jam the loose end against the hammer head. (It is a form of Blackwall Hitch.)

It will often be found more convenient to work on a splice if the wire is suspended horizontally at about chest height but, especially if the wire is a large one, the first round of tucks should be made with it held securely in a vice. It is often easier to drive a spike through a wire if the latter is resting on something solid.

When tucking one strand under another, try to avoid distorting the natural lay by tucking the end too close to the point where it emerges from under the previous strand. It is better to pass the spike under the strand where the tuck is to be made and then work it down the wire for a few centimetres with a spiral movement. Now pass the end through and work the spike back to its original position, at the same time pulling the strand through. Remove the spike and complete the job of pulling the strand tight. In any case, in wire splicing, never remove the spike from under a strand before you have passed the end through, even though in splicing hempen rope you can force a strand through without, perhaps, using a spike at all.

After making the first round of tucks, some people hold all the ends together along the standing part and beat the splice with a spike to make everything tight. This should not be done with any succeeding tucks, nor should the strands be hammered back as far as they will go. Rather, the second and following tucks should be allowed to lie in a long natural lay without being in any way loose.

In any splice, the end of the rope must be unlaid to a certain point in order to provide ends long enough to make the necessary tucks. With a fibre rope, a whipping at this point is not always necessary; with a wire rope it is essential. It should be about 5 cm long, made with rope yarn or, better still, marline, and should be put on away from the end of the rope. (A West Country Whipping will probably be found the easiest to make.)

Before cutting the whipping at the end of the rope and allowing the strands to unlay to the new one you have put on, however, put another light seizing about 20 cm from the end, unlay only to this, and then whip the end of each individual strand. If this is not done, each strand will open out and unlay when the end whipping is cut. Once the strand whippings are on, the temporary seizing can be removed.

With the strands apart and whipped individually, cut out the rope's fibre heart as far back as possible. If the strands have individual hearts, these, too, can be cut out one at a time, removing each whipping as needed and replacing it before you move on to the next strand. Cutting out the strand hearts is not essential, but it leads to a slimmer, neater and perhaps safer splice.

Do not be niggardly in the length you allow in ends for tucking. Short ends are harder to grip and bend. 60 cm should be sufficient for anything up to a 7.5-cm rope. Lastly, a splice weakens a wire rope by only 5% up to 19 mm diameter but on larger ropes the loss may be up to 30%.

2. Eye Splices

To TURN IN A THIMBLE. If the eye is to contain a thimble, lay
the grooved part of the latter on the rope with its fork on
the whipping which holds the unlaid strands. Then turn it
over along the rope once and mark where the fork now is.
Between this point and the whipping will be the portion of
rope that encloses the thimble and this should be served.
Now secure the crown of the thimble exactly to the centre of
the serving and, when it is fast, bend the rope round it in
the form of a loop, using the jaws of a vice to squeeze it
into shape if it is a large rope. Finally seize both sides of
the thimble between the crown and the fork to the rope to
hold it in place. (This whole operation can be performed
before the end whipping is cut and the strands unlaid, but
not before the whipping up to which they will be unlaid has
been put on.)

The inclusion or otherwise of a thimble makes no dif-
ference to the tucking.

To MAKE A LEFT-HANDED (NAVAL) SPLICE. (In this splice
and in those that follow, the ends are numbered in Arabic
numerals and the strands under which they are tucked in
Roman. In every case the numbering is as follows: When
the unlaid ends are spread out evenly in natural order, the
end on the extreme right is No. 1. Then, reading to the left,
come Nos. 2, 3, 4, 5 and 6, the extreme left-hand end. When
these ends are laid on the standing part of the rope with
their fork at the point where the splice is to commence,
the strand nearest to end No. 1 is strand I. Then, reading
to the left round the rope, come strands II, III, IV, V and
VI, which is I's right-hand neighbour.)

1. Tuck end No. 1 under strand I, 2 under II, 3 under
III, and 4 under IV, all tucks to be made from right to left.
2. Tuck end No. 6 under strands V and VI. *3.* Pull out the
spike only far enough to allow strand VI to drop down and
tuck end No. 5 under strand V. Every end now passes under
its own strand except end No. 6 which passes under two
strands, from right to left like the others. *4.* Haul and beat

the tucks tight (Fig. 134a). This completes the first set of tucks.

Some people cut the strand hearts out now before making the first tucks. A good rope yarn whipping may also be put over the completed tucks before proceeding to stage 5 in order to hold them in place whilst completing the splice.

5. Tuck all ends again twice, over one, under one, as in splicing hempen rope. 6. Lay back one-third of each end along the wire, stop these portions and make another set of tucks with the remaining two-thirds. 7. Similarly lay back and stop a second third and tuck the remainder of each strand. This tapers the splice off neatly (Fig. 134b). Cut off all ends and serve over the splice.

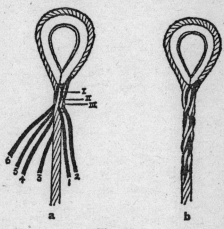

Fig. 134

TO MAKE A RIGHT-HANDED EYE SPLICE. This splice, sometimes called 'over and under' or 'Liverpool style', is popular in the merchant marine for it is quicker to make than a left-handed splice; but its use is frowned upon in the navy because it is not so strong. In any case, it should never be used on a wire that is liable to spin, e.g. in hoisting, as it might unlay.

1. Tuck end No. 1 under strands II and I (in that order)

from left to right. *2.* Drop strand I off the point of the spike and tuck end No. 2 under strand II from left to right. *3.* Tuck ends Nos. 3, 4, 5 and 6 also from left to right under II, IV, V and VI respectively. This completes the first set of tucks. *4.* Tuck again three times with full strands and twice with 'thirded' from left to right so that each end is always tucked under the same strand (in other words, so that it encircles it spirally). *5.* Cut off ends and serve.

To MAKE A LEFT-HANDED LOCKING SPLICE. As its name implies, this splice contains a 'lock' which helps to prevent the splice from drawing. *1.* Tuck end No. 1 under strand I from left to right. *2.* Tuck end No. 2 under strand II from right to left. *3.* Keeping the spike still under strand II, take end No. 6 underneath everything and tuck it under strand II from left to right. This makes the cross or lock. *4.* Tuck end No. 3 under strand III from right to left. *5.* Tuck end No. 5 under strands IV and V from right to left. *6.* Drop strand V off the point of the spike and tuck end No. 4 under strand IV from right to left. This completes the first set of tucks. *7.* Continue as for a simple left-handed splice with all tucks over one, under one, from right to left.

To MAKE A 3, 2 AND 1 SPLICE. This is another easily made, but not quite so strong, splice. *1.* Without injuring the fibre heart, insert the spike through the rope, entering between strands III and IV and emerging between strands I and VI. *2.* Pass end No. 1 through beside the spike, on the opposite side of it to the heart, which should be to the left of the spike. *3.* Drop strand I off the spike point and pass end No. 2 through to emerge between I and II. *4.* Drop strand II off the point and pass end No. 3 through to emerge between II and III. Three ends now enter through the centre but emerge from under different strands. *5.* Tuck 4 under IV, 5 under V and 6 under VI all from left to right. *6.* Continue as for a right-handed splice.

To MAKE A REDUCED EYE SPLICE. If, for some reason, an ordinary eye splice will be too bulky, a reduced splice might serve instead, but it is not, of course, so strong. *1.* Measure off enough rope to make an eye of the required size, plus the length of ends needed to make four tucks, and pass a stout whipping round it at this point. *2.* Unlay to this point and halve every strand and the heart. *3.* Relay six half strands (one from each whole strand) and half of the heart to form a reduced wire, and proceed as for a normal eye splice. The half-strands may be relaid by using your fingers, but a better method is to take a small flat piece of wood and in it bore six holes in a circle with a seventh at the centre. Pass one half-strand through each hole and the half-heart through the centre one and, by twisting the wood round and round, relay the wire.

3. Joining Two Wire Ropes

To MAKE A SHORT SPLICE. *1.* Put a firm, but narrow, whipping on both ropes about 45 cm from the end. *2.* Unlay to this point and cut out all hearts. *3.* Crutch the strands as for a Short Splice in hempen rope (except that there will be six to a side, not three). *4.* Put a firm seizing round the crutch to keep all parts in position whilst making the tucks. *5.* Tuck each strand over the strand from the other rope to its immediate left and under the one beyond it, again as in hempen rope splicing. *6.* Continue with two more full tucks and two 'thirded' ones on each rope, all left-handed, i.e. from right to left. *7.* Cut and pick away the whippings. *8.* Cut off all ends and serve.

A Short Splice cannot be used on a wire rope that has to pass through a block or pulley, as it is too bulky.

To MAKE A LONG SPLICE. As in hempen rope, a Long Splice should not increase the size of the wire and can therefore be used on a rope that has to pass through a block. However, it uses up a considerable amount of rope and it might be found more economical to obtain a new wire rather than to remove the weak portion of an old one with a Long Splice. In making wire rope slings (see Chapter 9) a Short Splice is usually employed, but if a continuous wire rope band without any bulges is needed, then a Long Splice must be used.

1. Unlay alternate strands of both ropes to a stout whipping for a distance which should be at least 3.6 m for a

2.5 cm rope, up to at least 9 m for a 7.5 cm and proportionate distances for intermediate sizes. This will leave three alternate strands on each rope unlaid and the other three still laid up round the heart. 2. Cut these latter threes and the hearts about 15 cm from the whippings. Each rope now has three long and three short ends. 3. Pull out the short lengths of heart and crutch the strands so that each long end is opposed to a short end of the other rope. 4. Stop the long ends of rope 'A' to the standing part of rope 'B' to keep them out of the way temporarily. 5. Cut off the whipping on rope 'A'. 6. Further unlay one short end of rope 'A' and lay up the corresponding long end of rope 'B' in its place until only about 90 cm of the long end remains. 7. Lock the two ends by crossing them and cut off the rope 'A' end until it, too, is only about 90 cm long. 8. Similarly unlay the other two rope 'A' short ends and lay up the rope 'B' ends in their places and lock them. 9. Cut the whipping on rope 'B' and lay the rope 'A' long ends up in place of the rope 'B' short ends and lock them.

The points of locking of opposing strands, i.e. the points up to which one strand is laid up in place of another, should be so arranged that they are equi-distant (Fig. 135). You may find that in the operation so far the assistance of at least one other person may be necessary, especially in crutching the strands tightly together, for if they are not so crutched an unsightly join will result.

Fig. 135

Wire rope strands cannot be hitched, unfortunately, so the problem now arises of burying the ends in such a way that the strands will bind round them and hold them in position. This means that the hearts will have to be pulled out to make a space for the ends, but since the outside strands will not grip on the smooth surface of a buried wire, the ends must first be parcelled over with thin cloth or served with thin yarns. Further, they must each be cut to the exact length so that each, when buried, butts against the end of the one next to it. If two ends are too short so that they do not meet, the outer strands will sag into the empty space; if they are too long and overlap, the wire will bulge.

To bury the ends. 1. Pull out the heart of rope 'A' to a point just past the first pair of locked ends. (Running a spike along between the strands where the heart is emerging will make it easier to pull the latter out.) 2. Uncross the lock. 3. Insert the spike under the strand next to this first loose end of rope 'A' and pass the point of the spike over that end. 4. Now, by moving the spike along the rope towards the initial crutching point and at the same time bearing down with its point on the loose end, the latter will be found to disappear into the space left by the heart. 5. Pull more of the heart out until it is over half-way towards the next pair of locked ends. 6. Using the spike as in stages 3 and 4, but this time moving away from the crutch, bury the loose end of rope 'B' previously locked with the rope 'A' loose end already buried. 7. Pull out more heart and bury the next loose end of rope 'A', then that of rope 'B', then the third of rope 'A' and the third of rope 'B'. 8. Cut off the heart of rope 'A' and push the end into the rope. 9. Repeat stages 1 to 8 on rope 'B'. 10. A little hammering and twisting will put the rope back into shape again, and the splice should be almost impossible to detect. An alternative method is not to uncross the lock as in stage 2, but to bury the ends using two spikes as shown in the illustration (Fig. 136).

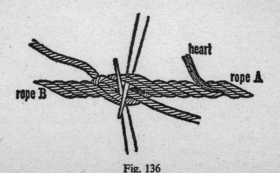

Fig. 136

TO MAKE A WIRE GROMMET. *1.* Extract a strand from a flexible steel wire rope equal in length to five and a half to six times the circumference of the desired grommet. If the finished ring is to be served, remember that this will reduce the inside circumference of the grommet and that the actual ring of wire will therefore need to be slightly larger. *2.* Towards one end of the strand, form a loop of the required size and half knot the ends, taking care to preserve the natural lay of the strand, i.e. if it is from a right-handed rope, then the right-hand end must be twisted over the left-hand and vice versa if it is from a left-handed rope. *3.* Dog the longer end a number of times round the loop, keeping it in the natural curves of the lay, and then check that the loop is still the correct size. *4.* The long end must now be dogged round and round the loop to make five complete circuits (as in making a grommet with hempen rope, except that there only three complete circuits are made). After making the third circuit, it may be found that using a pricker or small spike will help to put the fourth properly into place, and the fifth circuit should be lightly hammered at every turn to lay the strand well in. *5.* Finish off this five-part grommet in one of the following ways: (a) if the grommet is to be parcelled and served, simply cut the ends off short so that they butt together; or (b) bury the ends as in long splicing so that they finally butt together on the opposite side of the grommet to the original half knot (this will give the five strands a heart); or (c) halve each end, cross them and dispose of them by tucking over one and under one.

You may have noticed that, whereas a hempen rope grommet has three parts just as a hempen rope has three strands, the wire rope grommet described above has only five parts, not six. When you make one, you will find that there is no room left for a sixth part. Nevertheless, the five-part grommet is widely and commonly used, although its strength should be taken as only about three-quarters of that of a flexible wire rope of the same diameter.

By taking more trouble, however, it is possible to make a six-part grommet with a single strand of wire. *1.* Carry out stages *1* to *4* as above but use a strand equal in length to about eight times the circumference of the desired grommet. *2.* After the fifth part has been laid in, take another strand of the same size equal in length to the grommet's circumference plus a few centimetres and, with a pricker, work this into the centre of the five parts already laid up as a heart, leaving both ends sticking out. *3.* Now that the grommet has a heart, it will be found that there is room to lay in a sixth circuit with the original strand. Do this. *4.* Tuck both ends of the original strand through the grommet with three parts on either side of them. *5.* Pull out the temporary heart and lay up the ends in its place (as Long Splicing). *6.* Cut them off so that they butt on the opposite side of the grommet.

PART III
Making Things

CHAPTER EIGHTEEN

ROPE LADDERS

A Climbing Rope

The rope can be of any length but should, for safety, have a breaking strength of at least 909 kg (2000 lbs). Generally a natural-fibre rope will offer a better gripping surface. The bottom end should be fused, whipped or spliced into an eye; the top fused or whipped for securing round a beam, bough, etc. with a Round Turn and Two Half-hitches, with the end stopped to the standing part for greater security – or eye-spliced if it will be suspended from a hook.

To make climbing easier, at every 30 cm up from the bottom eye pass two lengths of cord through the rope under adjoining strands and with the four ends fashion a Diamond Knot round the rope. These knots will provide hand- and foot-holds. To greatly improve these holds, make truncated cones of oak, 5 cm deep, bored vertically through the centre with holes just large enough to take the rope. Slip one such cone down on each Diamond Knot, which will support it.

A Strong, Light Ladder

Use rungs of wooden dowelling or aluminium tubing 2.5 cm in diameter and 40 cm in length, grooved at either end, and a length of rope equal to more than twice the drop required, allowing for length above the top rung for securing purposes. For strength with lightness, the best rope would be an 8 mm Polypropylene.

1. Middle the rope and make an eye by seizing both parts together. (Here and elsewhere, use a strong twine of the same material as the rope itself.) *2.* 30 cm up from the eye insert the first rung *through* both parts of the rope until 10 mm is projecting on either side. Use a fid to open the strands, being careful not to damage them, and twist to close when the rung is inserted. *3.* Insert further rungs at measured 30-cm intervals. *4.* Fuse or eye-splice the top end of each part of the rope.

5. Lay out or, better, hang up the ladder to check that rungs are evenly spaced and horizontal. Adjustments can be made by rolling the end of a rung along between the strands.

6. Put a tight lashing of strong twine on either end of each rung as follows: (i) Put a small Running Bowline on the rung *inside* the ladder. (ii) Take one full turn round the rung *outside* the ladder. (iii) Take one full turn round the rope *above* the rung. (iv) Take a *half* turn round the rung *outside* the ladder, followed by a full turn round the rope *below* the rung. (v) Take a full turn round the rung *inside* the ladder. (vi) Repeat all turns. (vii) Finish with a Constrictor Knot or Clove Hitch *inside* the ladder.

7. Put palm-and-needle whippings on the rope for 5 cm on either side of every rung, and over-stitch as in Snaking (see Chapter Two).

8. If the rungs are of aluminium tubing, the ends may be bunged. Make the bottom two or three bungs at least removable so that if the ladder is lowered into water they will flood and sink. This will enable anyone in the water to get his/her feet on to a rung. In a yacht the ladder can be secured, rolled up at the rail, by a slip knot with a long loose end left dangling to water-level so that anyone falling overboard can release the ladder simply by pulling on the cord.

A HEAVIER, TOUGHER LADDER

Nowadays the Pilot or Jack Ladder used by ships for picking up or dropping personnel to a boat usually has metal rungs and wire or chain supports. It can, however, also be made with wooden rungs and rope. For rope, use two lengths each of more than twice the length of drop required and with a breaking strength of 2720 kg. For rungs use stout planks 45 x 15 cm drilled with four holes, two at either end 3.7 cm in and 5 cm apart.

1. Middle one rope and thread it through holes at the *opposite ends* of each plank. Similarly thread the other rope. Each rope goes down through one side of the rungs and up through the other. *2.* Below the lowest rung, bring all four parts of rope together and seize them into an eye that should be served all round. *3.* Secure the lowest rung 30 cm up from the eye by putting tight Round Seizings (see Chapter Ten) round each pair of ropes both below and above the rung. *4.* Similarly secure the other rungs at 30-cm intervals. *5.* Finish by short-splicing together the tops of each pair of ropes. These can then be seized into eyes if desired.

This ladder can also be rolled up when not in use but will make a bulkier bundle than the light ladder previously described. It can also be made with wire ropes (and with metal rungs, provided they are punched with the necessary holes) as described for rope, but the seizings will need to be put on with seizing wire (see Chapter Seventeen).

CHAPTER NINETEEN

NETS

Netting has a wide variety of uses: in the garden, afloat, on a car roof-rack for covering loose objects, as carrying bags and keep-nets; on the sports field and in playgrounds. For the handy-person who wants to make his/her own nets, the basic techniques are not difficult to learn.

Before starting on a net decide what is needed in (a) shape; (b) overall size; (c) the size of the meshes; and (d) strength. The last-named will decide the twine, cord or rope from which a net is made, e.g. a climbing net for children will demand stronger cordage than a bag for carrying, say, footballs. Mesh-size is also important: a gardener's bean-net may have meshes 15 cm square; in an angler's keep-net they will be of only a finger's width. Whatever the cordage or mesh-size, however, the basic techniques and equipment are the same.

The equipment is simple. First, cordage; lots of it, for this is what makes the net. Secondly, a shuttle: a suitably sized piece of smooth wood, longer than it is wide, on which the cord can be wound longitudinally for easing passing whilst making knots, and easy freeing when more cord is required. One shape for a shuttle is shown in Figure 137. The size used will depend upon the requirements of a particular net in mesh and cord sizes.

Thirdly, but not always essential, a gauge: a thin, flat piece of wood, possibly slightly oval in cross-section, whose width is equal to the length of *one side* of the mesh to be made. Thus a mesh 7.5 cm square requires a 7.5-cm-wide gauge. However, it is very much easier to use your own fingers as a gauge, provided you know how wide they are. The average adult finger is about 20 mm wide, so that all four will make a 7.5-cm gauge, whilst just one will serve in making a small-mesh keep-net.

Many nets can be made seated at an old table or board into which nails can be driven, but with larger nets it is better to work with the net suspended from a headrope with room to work from both sides, for at the end of each row of meshes it is necessary either to turn your work over or to carry on from the other side. Most people find it easier

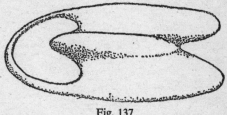

Fig. 137

always to work from left to right on a net, and the directions in this chapter are based on that practice. If you find that you have to work from right to left, reverse all the directions given.

It helps to have readily available scissors, a raffia needle, good light and a chair.

Craft shops and chandlers stock a variety of possible cordages, including twines already coloured. If you want to dye cotton twine yourself, do so before you make your net, otherwise it may shrink later. Slippery synthetic cords are less easy to net but bonded Nylon is satisfactory.

The meshes in a net are either diamond-shaped or square-shaped. The former leave zig-zag edges, the latter straight edges, but the former are somewhat simpler to make.

To Make a Diamond-mesh Net

1. Fill your shuttle with netting cord. Wind it on carefully and evenly, allowing the ball of cordage to rotate freely so that no kinks are wound on.

2. Drive in two large nails slightly further apart than the width of the net to be made.

3. Knot a length of cord stronger than the netting cord into a continuous loop just large enough to slip over the two nails.

4. Make an Overhand Knot in the end of the netting cord, leaving a good length of 'tail'.

5. Pass the shuttle up *through the left-hand end* of the headrope loop, leaving the Overhand Knot below it, and pinch in place with your left hand to hold it there.

6. Throw a bight of netting cord over the headrope and bring the shuttle up behind the headrope but through the bight and pull taut.

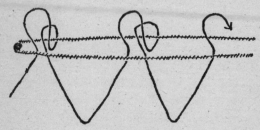

Fig. 138

7. Hold the gauge (or the necessary number of fingers) close under the headrope and bring the shuttle down *in front* of it, then up behind it and finally through the headrope to repeat stage *6.*

8. Repeat stages *6* and *7* to form the required number of meshes along one side of your net.

9. Lift the headrope off the nails and turn it over, end for end, if you have it on a board; or walk round to the other side if you have it suspended.

10. Holding the gauge/fingers close to the bottom of what is now the left-hand mesh in the first row, bring the shuttle down in front of it, then up behind it, and pass it from behind through the extreme left-hand mesh.

11. With your left thumb and forefinger holding the cord tightly in position where it enters the mesh, throw a bight of cord from the shuttle over your left hand.

12. Pass the shuttle to the right, round behind the mesh and then down through it, from front to back.

13. Still pinching the cord in place, pull the shuttle cord and work the knot tight. You will now have made a Netting Knot (otherwise called a Sheet Bend or Weaver's Knot), the basis of all net-making. To make it accurately without losing control of the gauge and where the cord enters the mesh above requires practice, but once you have mastered it you will be able to net quickly.

14. Repeat stages *12* and *13* to complete the row of meshes.

15. Turn your work over, end to end (or walk round) and repeat stages *12, 13, 14* and *15* until you have completed the required number of rows. (For a net square in shape this will be the same as the number of meshes you fashioned in stage *8*.)

16. Cut the cord off the shuttle, leaving enough end to make an Overhand Knot which should be worked tight up against the last Netting Knot. Cut the end off close.

17. Return to the 'tail' left in stage *4*, netting-knot it to the mesh immediately below it and finish as in stage *16*.

TO PUT A DOUBLE SELVAGE ROUND THE NET

1. Rewind your shuttle with *two* cords.

2. Using the two cords as one, tie a Netting Knot on to any perimeter mesh on the net but leave tails on both cords, one at least 15 cm long, the other at least 30 cm long.

3. Work round the perimeter using the gauge/fingers and tying Netting Knots with both cords as one.

4. Finish by cutting the cords off the shuttle so that you can join each to a 'tail' tight up against the existing Netting Knots in adjoining meshes.

TO JOIN ON NEW CORD WHEN REFILLING THE SHUTTLE use a Fisherman's Knot (see Chapter Four) positioned so that it is tight against an existing Netting Knot and will not be noticed. When refilling with two cords, position the knots against consecutive Netting Knots, not the same one.

INCREASING AND DECREASING

You can *increase* the width of your net at any stage by netting-in extra meshes in a row. Take the cord round the gauge/fingers and through the mesh above *twice*, instead of once, before making the Netting Knot. When increasing by only one mesh at a time, do this at the beginning of a row; when by two, at the beginning and end. To *decrease*, take the cord through *two* adjoining meshes in the row above before making the Netting Knot round both of them.

CYLINDRICAL NETS

To make a cylindrical net (e.g. a keep-net, basketball net, carrying bag, etc.). Start with a ring of plastic, metal, wood or rope of the size required for the neck of the net. (The material used will depend upon the purpose of the net.) If the neck is to be closable by a drawstring, make this first – as a continuous loop of rope with the ends tied or spliced together – and use this as the starting ring. Then:

1. Tie a stopper Overhand Knot in the end of the netting cord.
2. Tie the end of the cord to the ring with a Clove Hitch.
3. With the gauge/fingers against the ring, bring the cord down in front, then up behind and tie another Clove Hitch on the ring.
4. Repeat stage *3* all round the ring, making the Clove Hitches the same distance apart as the width of the gauge/fingers.
5. Using the gauge/fingers and netting-knotting, make second and successive rows of meshes until the cylinder has reached the required depth. Finish off if the cylinder is to be open-bottomed, e.g. basketball.
6. Decrease by two or more meshes in a row until only two meshes are left, if the cylinder is to be closed.
7. Netting-knot these two together and make an Overhand Knot worked up tight to act as a stopper.

In a keep-net, one, two or three additional inflexible rings can now be inserted at different levels inside the cylinder, to which they should be secured by a succession of Clove Hitches.

A basketball net should be constructed on an iron ring with an inside diameter of 45 cm. The top row of netting should contain ten mesh, using a 15-cm gauge. For the next three rows, use a 3.7-cm gauge. 4.5 m of twine will be needed.

A draw-string carrying-bag can usefully be increased by one mesh per row for up to ten rows and then similarly decreased to the finish.

To make a Square-mesh Net

Square meshes, as opposed to diamonds poised on a point, make a straight-edged net, either square, if the number of meshes along each side is the same, or oblong. Before starting calculate the number of meshes you will need along each side by dividing the side length by the mesh size. Thus a net that is to be 3 m long by 1.5 wide with 2.5-cm-square meshes will need 3 m divided by 2.5 cm equals 120 meshes on its long sides; and 1.5 m divided by 2.5 cm equals 60 meshes on its short sides. A climbing net 3 m square with 30-cm-square meshes will have ten meshes per side.

Start by making a *short* side as follows:

1. Hang a loop of cord on a nail.
2. Tie the shuttle cord to this loop with a Clove Hitch, leaving a short 'tail'.
3. Using the gauge/fingers make two meshes netting-knotted into the working loop as for a diamond-mesh net. (This will be one corner of your net.)
4. Turn your work over (or walk round) and make another row of two meshes.
5. Increase this to three meshes by knotting again into the right-hand mesh above but *this time go the wrong way round,* i.e. instead of throwing a bight to the left and passing the shuttle round from right to left, throw the bight to the right and pass the shuttle round from left to right.
6. Repeat stages 4 and 5 increasing with a 'wrong way round' knot on each row until you have completed rows equivalent to the number of meshes in your 'short' side (e.g. 60 in the net instanced above).
7. If your net is to be square in shape, continue netting-knotting as before but in each row *decrease* by one mesh by knotting the last two meshes together with a 'wrong way round' knot.

8. When only two meshes are left, plus the shuttle cord, work a Netting Knot through both together, pull tight and add an Overhand Knot as a stopper.

9. Remove the loop from its nail, untie it and pull free from the net.

10. Use the initial short 'tail' left to tie the first two meshes together as for the last two in stage *8*.

If your net is to be oblong in shape, from stage *7* continue netting-knotting without either increasing or decreasing until you have added rows equivalent to the number of meshes in your 'long' side (which, for a tennis net, will be 280!). Then start decreasing as in stages *7* to *10*.

The sides of your net can be strengthened by clove-hitching a perimeter cord to every Netting Knot round the outside of the net. If making a tennis, badminton or volley-ball net, secure a strong rope or wire to the top long side of the net with Clove Hitches, one for every Netting Knot, and then cover with a doubled canvas strip, the two sides of which should be sewn together through the net. A sail-maker's palm and needle will make this task easier. Along the bottom of the net, another tensioning cord can either be laced through the lowest row of meshes or secured to it by Clove Hitches. This, too, can be given an enclosing canvas strip.

A good exercise in net-making is to make a square net of 24 square meshes per side, using a 3.7-cm gauge and strong seaming twine or 36g cotton twine. This net can be tensioned across a tubular or wooden frame by a strong spring at each corner with the frame mounted to tilt slightly backwards. This will provide an excellent 'bounce back' net for catching practice. Brightly coloured yarns or tape woven into the centre will make a target at which to aim.

NET DIMENSIONS:

Tennis : 10.9 m by 91 cm; tensioned so that it is 106.6 cm high at the posts and 91 cm high at the centre. The top edge should be covered with a 7.5 cm wide white tape doubled over. Use a 3.7-cm gauge and 610 m of strong twine. Size: 288 meshes by 28 meshes.

Badminton : 6 m by 76 cm; tensioned so that it is 1.54 m high at the posts and 1.52 m high at the centre. The top edge should be covered with a white canvas strip. Use a 19-mm gauge and 518 m of strong twine. Size: 320 meshes by 40 meshes.

Volleyball : 9.4 m by .98 m with a double thickness of white canvas or linen 5 cm wide stretched across the top; tensioned so that it is 2.43 metres high (men) or 2.24 m (women). The mesh must be 4″ square. Removable bands of white material to be fixed to the net above and perpendicular to the court's sidelines. Use a 10-cm gauge and 213 m of strong twine. Size: 94 meshes by 10 meshes.

CHAPTER TWENTY

ODD JOBS

TYING A PARCEL

1. Take the string once round the parcel and tie a Clove Hitch on the standing part (Fig. 139a). *2.* With one hand hold this knot firmly on to the centre of the parcel and with the other pull the string tight. *3.* Lead the string off to left or right, turn the parcel over and tuck a bight under the string already running across the back of the parcel (Fig. 139b). *4.* Pull on the bight to tighten. *5.* Pinching the cross-strings to keep them tight, tuck the end of the string through the bight and pull tight. *6.* Turn the parcel over again and finish with two or three Half Hitches. *7.* If the parcel is large and needs extra turns, start with a Clove Hitch on any string and then continue with stages *3* to *6*.

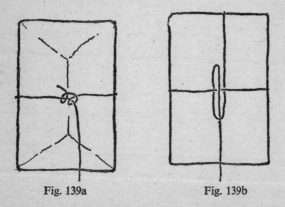

Fig. 139a   Fig. 139b

LOWERING A HEAVY WEIGHT FROM A LADDER

Householders occasionally find that they need to lower a

heavy weight whilst working up a ladder, e.g. in removing a chimney pot or a length of cast-iron drainpipe. Provided that the ladder is in sound condition, the top or next-to-top rung can be used as a pulley. *1.* Fasten the rope securely round the object to be lowered. If the object is oblong or roughly so in shape, use a Running Bowline, which will tighten under the weight, with steadying turns at right-angles to this. If it is cylindrical, use a Rolling Hitch with an extra steadying Half Hitch (see Timber Hitch, Chapter Three, Figure 21). *2.* Lead the rope over the rung from the wall side towards you and secure two or three rungs lower down with a Clove Hitch taken with the bight. You can now concentrate on freeing the object until its weight is taken by the rope, which, because of its lead, will be pulling the ladder into the wall and thus holding it steady. *3.* Holding the tensioned rope below the 'pulley' rung with one hand, with the other free the Clove Hitch and take the weight with both hands. *4.* Lower the object by allowing the rope to render round the 'pulley' rung under control.

It is possible to hoist an object, provided it is not too heavy, by reversing the above stages. Keep on all hitches until the object is firmly fixed into position.

Towing a Car

No matter how carefully the towing vehicle is driven, some shock-loading is bound to be imposed on the tow-rope. If, then, you can use Nylon rope, so much the better. Secure the rope to the special towing fitment, if any, or to a body member but not to the suspension or round an axle. The best securing hitch is a Round Turn and Two Half Hitches, but do not leave a long end that might become entangled somewhere.

Making a Hammock

The 'bed' of a hammock can be of stout material, e.g. canvas, or of stout twine or rope. It is suspended at either end by clews, lines that come together, fanwise, at a ring that can be hooked directly on to a support or be fitted with a length of rope, called a lanyard, for securing round a bough, beam, deckhead hook or whatever.

The 'bed' can be of any size to suit personal taste but standard is 1.8 m long by .9 m wide. The clews should be at least 30 cm long. For sunbathing and simple lazing, the 'bed' is best kept open by a spreader at each end, but for sleeping it is better left unspread, when it will close round its occupant snugly and comfortably.

The clews should be of 5 mm diameter, three-strand white hemp or synthetic rope of comparable strength (e.g. 4 mm Polyethylene). The rings should be of 6-mm steel, 9 cm in diameter. The lanyards, if used, can be of any rope with a breaking strength of at least 910 kg.

To make a canvas 'bed'. 1. Cut a sheet of material 1.9 m by .96 m. (This is for a 1.8 m x .9 m hammock. For one of any other size, add or substract the differences.) *2.* On the long sides fold back 2.5 cm hem and stitch securely. *3.* On the short sides fold back 7.5 cm of material and stitch securely with two lines of strong seaming twine 3.7 cm apart so as to leave a 'tunnel' at each end of the 'bed' into which a spreader can be pushed. *4.* Between the two lines of stitching punch or cut holes (12 for a .9 m-wide hammock or 16 for a 1.06 m-wide hammock) evenly spaced and just large enough to take metal or plastic eyelets of 6 mm diameter.

To make the clews: 1. Cut your clew line into 1.2 m lengths. *2.* Secure to one ring the same number of lengths as you have made eyelet holes in one end of the 'bed' (e.g. 12 or 16). Use either Clove Hitches or, for a neater and more permanent job, Eye Splices. *3.* Divide the clews into four groups of three (or four, if you have sixteen). *4.* Plait each group into a tight Flat Sennit (see Chapter Fifteen) 15 cm long. *5.* Starting with the central clews, tie each into its corresponding hole at one end of the 'bed'. Take the clew down through the eyelet and secure on to its own standing part with two Half Hitches. For the two central clews, the distance from ring to eyelet should be at least .9 m. If the hammock is to have a spreader this should be inserted *before* the clews are tied.

6. Make and tie on the clews at the other end of the hammock. *7.* Suspend the hammock by both ends and adjust the lengths of the clews until all are equally bearing the strain. If the hammock has spreaders the clew lengths will increase progressively from the centre outwards, but if it is not to have spreaders, i.e. is to be used as a bed without quotes, the clew lengths should *decrease* progressively outwards until the outside lines are 3.7 cm shorter than those at the centre. *8.* When you are satisfied that every clew length is correct, tighten the Half Hitches and either cut off loose ends or stop them to their standing parts, which would be preferable with synthetic ropes.

To secure the lanyards : Into each ring eye-splice a lanyard, the other end of which should be whipped or fused. When slinging a hammock by a lanyard, it is best to take the latter over the securing position (e.g. hook, beam, bough) and bring it back to tie on to the ring with a Double Sheet Bend. If it is not long enough for this, use a Round Turn and Two Half Hitches on the securing position, or if the latter is vertical (e.g. a pole or mast) a Rolling Hitch.

To make a netting hammock 'bed' : This should not be made without a spreader. Use No. 72 cotton seine twine or 5-ply flax roping twine and a 3.7-cm gauge (or, possibly, three fingers – see Chapter Nineteen).

1. Hang up one spreader to serve as a headrope.

2. Tie an Overhand Knot with a long 'tail' in the netting twine and then make a Clove Hitch on the left-hand end of the spreader, leaving the Overhand Knot just below it.

3. With the gauge close up under the spreader bring the twine round it to make, in succession, eleven more Clove Hitches, finishing near the right-hand end of the spreader. Turn your work end to end.

4. Turning your work at the end of each row, make successive rows of meshes as follows:

  (a) Up to Row 11 – twelve meshes
  (b) On Row 12 increase by one
  (c) On Row 14 increase by two
  (d) On Row 15 increase by one (This row will have sixteen meshes)
  (e) Work straight through to Row 22

   (f) On Row 23 decrease by two

   (g) On Row 25 decrease by one

   (h) On Row 29 decrease by one (This row will have twelve meshes)

   (i) Work straight to Row 40 and tie off

   (j) Knot the initial 'tail' into the mesh below it.

5. Secure the second spreader to the last row of meshes with Clove Hitches.

6. Secure the clews to the 'bed' as described above except that instead of passing through an eyelet each will pass through a mesh and round the spreader.

In the pattern given above the first spreader is intended to be at the head of the hammock and the second at the foot. If you want the latter slung higher than the former, make the foot clews 30 cm shorter than the head clews or adjust the lengths of the head and foot lanyards.

TO MAKE A NETTING 'SHELF': Where stowage space is restricted (e.g. in a tent or cabin) a 'mini-hammock' makes a useful, and easily rolled up, shelf.

1. For each spreader, use a piece of wood 30 cm long and no more than 2.5 cm wide. The twine used will depend on the strength you require.

2. Using one spreader as a headrope and one finger as a gauge, make a diamond-mesh net of 12 meshes in a row, 36 rows long.

3. Tie the other spreader to the last row with Clove Hitches.

4. To each spreader tie a cord at least 60 cm long by Clove Hitches at either end of the spreader. These will be the slinging lanyards.

If made with coloured cords and twines and with the spreaders painted, this 'netting shelf' can be decorative as well as functional.

TO MAKE A HALTER FOR A COW OR SHEEP

1. Make a small loop in the end of the rope.

2. Pull a bight of the standing part through the loop. This will create two nooses, of which the pulled-through bight should be the smaller.

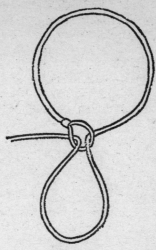

Fig. 140

3. Slip the larger noose over the animal's head and the smaller over its muzzle (Fig. 140).

To make a halter for a horse

Fig. 141

1. Make a Bowline Loop large enough to go over the horse's head, with the knot under its neck.

2. Make two Half Hitches round its muzzle, the second higher up than the first (Fig. 141).

3. Pull the second Half Hitch through the first and lift it over the horse's head to the point on the neck where the Bowline loop rests (Fig. 141).

INDEX